LET WATER FIND ITS OWN WAY

My Keys to Success In Life

OTTAVIO DEVIVO

This book is dedicated to my wife, Anna,
for all her love and support;
and to my children, Francine, John, and Thomas
for all the happiness they have given me.

Acknowledgments

Many thanks to Carol Bennett for her guidance and her endless hours of transcribing. Also thanks to my good friend, Rob Morgan, for his tireless efforts for the art work on the cover, and Michelle DeVivo for the photo assistance. Special thanks to Lou Romeo and Iris Romeo, their insight demonstrates the strong bonds in our family. Thanks also to Rick Greco for the Italian translation.

"Lascia Che L'Acqua Trovi La Sua Strada"

(Let The Water Find Its Own Way)

The above quote that eventually became translated into English for the title of this book was a saying that the author heard his father, Tommaso, use many times while growing up. He used it to describe his way of dealing with family, friends, and life in general. His father believed that many problems in life could resolve themselves when left to follow their own path of least resistance, and not meddled with through human interference.

What the author found in reflecting on his own life in this book was that many of the situations that he himself encountered were successfully overcome by his application of this simple yet profoundly powerful philosophy of his dear departed father.

— RM

Introduction

Ottavio DeVivo is a successful and well-regarded maker of fine furniture in New Rochelle, New York. *Born in Serino, Italy, he emigrated to the U.S. in 1966 where he continued the trade of his father, who was also a furniture maker. Ottavio's New Rochelle store was established in 1977 and continues to produce custom-designed furniture.*

What follows are transcribed conversations with Ottavio, conducted over the span of more than a dozen years. They capture in detail much about his remarkable life, but more importantly, they share with us his reflections and recollections about his parents, his wife and his children and how family values are lived, not just spoken, and how the American Dream, in his case, was realized.

Ottavio has put three children through college and prospered in business. He has a vacation home in Florida. He is a happy man, but his journey wasn't easy. Lessons from his father and the example of his loving mother gave him a foundation, but friends who helped him when he arrived in the U.S. and the girl he married had a lot to do with his success. He was persuaded to share his experiences and conclusions in this book.

It is a testament to family values, lived not just spoken, and perseverance. He also shows how we can help immigrants today who arrive without English, but with a dream of something more than they left in their home country.

— CB

CHAPTER ONE

Growing up in Serino

They called me Ottavio because I was the eighth child born to Tommaso and Assunta DeVivo in the small Italian town of Serino. It was a beautiful town with maybe 10,000 people. Actually, I was born June 6, 1937 in San Biagio, a part of Serino, which is in the province of Avellino. What I remember most, from about the time I was five, is my Mamma, because she was so kind. She was a beautiful person. And one of the best parts I remember was every morning when she used to wash everybody, put us together with nice clothes on and say, "Go play." We had a small, very small yard.

I remember running outside with the chickens, because they ran all around the house. I was a little bit faster. I used to play with my brother and he would push me all around in a wagon. I never forget little simple things. We had a little wagon that my father made with three wheels. I was arguing with him that we should build another wheel. Anyway, it was wonderful, these things I remember.

Tommaso DeVivo and Assunta DeVivo

We had a friend, our neighbor. I'll never forget this nice boy named Umberto. He came from a family of eight or nine brothers, no girls in the family. And we became very close. I used to get food in my kitchen and bring it to him, not because he didn't have it, but because we traded the food that my mother made: like a special bread, that was excitement for the little kids. The beautiful thing was we had nice neighbors all around.

Things weren't too good, not like now where everybody has everything. It was wartime in Italy and I remember when we used to eat a little piece of cheese, we really appreciated it because the piece of cheese on the table was not too big. Anyway, we still had fun.

I remember in our church there was this priest. His name was Padre (Don) Gaetano Tedeschi. He was calling on me all the time, because I was the one that always got in trouble. A lot of times I gave him a problem. Actually, the problem wasn't me because, when I was in church, there was a girl that talked, used to play around, things like that. I used to push her and she would scream. Then the Padre would yell at me.

Tommaso standing in front of family house in Serino

Don Gaetano organized the Boy Scouts and I was part of the Boy Scouts. We had about 15 boys. Every Saturday we would get together. He was very kind. My mother was very happy. In this way, we went to the church, learned things, better things, and were in good company; but most important, I was really happy. I was about 10 years old, maybe 12, and being a Boy Scout was a big thing. Sometimes the Boy Scouts met near the town. There was a small piece of land where we used to go to practice lighting fires. The priest was so happy with us, and we were happy too. One time, when we little boys got bigger, we decided we wanted to go away. My friends and I loved climbing mountains. When we were about 13, we organized a trip, but the priest said we had to ask our parents if they would give their O.K. We wanted to go out for three or four days, but knew, if we asked our parents they would say no. They wouldn't want us to take chances sleeping in the mountains, things like that. It was too far away.

Ottavio and Reverend Don Gaetano Tedeschi
(Ottavio is first on the left side with Don Gaetano next to him)

Well, anyway, two of my friends and I decided to go by ourselves. We took a chance. I was a little bit wild. I did the wrong thing because I didn't tell my mother and father.

We went up the mountain, Monte Terminio, and then we went to sleep in a small tent. We gave a big worry to our families, and a big problem for the priest. Our mothers and fathers went to the priest asking where did they go? They blamed him. But we were all fine. What I remember most was another boy, he wanted to come too. He asked his father and his father didn't give him the O.K., but then he left the next day. He found us.

All we did was just light a fire and sleep in a little tent. It was a little bit dangerous, but we didn't do anything else. We were safe. When we came back, my mother was so happy, but the priest yelled at us that we can't do such a thing. Anyway, the time went a little faster this way. This was the excitement at the time.

Monte Terminio

We went to school and then came back from school. Then we went to the church to see the priest. He taught us many different things, and then we ran and played in the church yard. The biggest thing that I remember was that my mother and father wanted us home for dinner all the time. During the day, my father was at work, but at 12 o'clock, he came home for dinner. This was family time. We had a big family, and we would eat altogether.

On Saturdays Mamma used to make this special chicken soup with a little spaghetti and chicken. It was delicious. The big excitement at the dinner table, was everybody stealing food one from the other. My mamma loved it. My father, I'll never forget, would sit at the table with a glass of wine and smile. He was so happy! Now that I have my own family, I realize why he was so happy. Dinner was noisy but beautiful.

∻

My father had a brother, my Zio Francesco, who never got married, and he lived with us. He was a second father for us. When I was a little boy, five years old, the American soldiers came to liberate Italy from the Germans. My father was in the army, so my uncle took care of us. He took all the family to this big train tunnel. When the Americans bombed the town in 1942, we were in the bottom of this tunnel. Everyday my uncle used to go out to get chickens and bring us food. We survived there for a few weeks. During that time, I started having a pain in my leg, and cried a lot. I don't know what it was. The doctor said later maybe polio. I was sick for almost one year and my mother worried...she became very attached to me. I don't remember much more. Thank God, after a while, I was all right. The leg was fine. I was ok, I played soccer, climbed mountains.

My uncle really took care of the family. Even when my

father came back from the army, he continued to help the family. He was a special man. I will never forget him. He was the guard for the family. It was like having two fathers.

After the war, when my father came home, he concentrated on his work. He used to take care of some land for a very wealthy man in town. When he came home he told us how that when he was in the army, he sometimes used to make cabinets and fix furniture for the army officers. It's amazing. When I think about that, I think about my own time in the army, when I did the same thing. My father was a very simple man, very simple.

Tommaso and Assunta's headboard, hand carved by Tommaso

My father worked two or three jobs. He would build a cabinet like you cannot believe. He would cut down a tree and with that wood he would then make furniture. I remember once he created a beautiful door for the front of this big church. He took me with him because the door had to fit perfect so the lock would work. He took me with him on his jobs a lot. I loved working with him. At night when he used to get paid, he'd bring home food to feed everybody. Many times he was also paid in food. Some people were so rich, they had so much food, so he would bring it home. This was always a special meal.

He raised ten kids. I'll never forget the way he worked all his life. He had great hands. God gave him, very big, strong hands. He never was afraid to lift things. When I was with him, we'd joke around. He loved me. He loved all the kids.

℞

One day, my father took me into his shop. He had a little shop, and I was doing something, working on this machine. My father saw blood on the floor and said "What happened?" This machine was running so fast, I had no pain, but I lost the ends of two fingers. Anyway, I'll never forget, he took me to the doctor, the small town doctor, who was a friend of the family. When he saw my hand, this doctor fainted.

My father made a bandage out of some rags and we went to the hospital, to the emergency room. When we went into the emergency room, the other doctor wanted to cut my two fingers off to the joint, but my father was so upset. He then took me to a relative, Dr. Aristito De Vivo. He took good care of me. It took months for my fingers to heal, but I kept the joints.

Tommaso's shop in Serino

☙

Altogether in my family, there are five sisters and five brothers. I was 13 years old when my third sister, Gaetana, got engaged to a very handsome man. His name was Pasquale. He had a very complicated character, but I liked him and he liked me. All the time when he came to my house I would make him feel very good. I'd give him a compliment, I always told a joke. I was the only one that made him feel at home. He was an educated man. He had some degree. I don't remember in what, but he didn't have a job. My father used to say, "What do you do for a living?" He'd reply, "One day, I'm gonna get a good job." My sister really loved him. He didn't want anything from anybody. He didn't want any favors. One day, my father couldn't take it any more because they wanted to get married. My father said "What are you going to do without a job?" So, my father took him to see a politician friend in Rome for whom my father had done a lot of work. They called my father "Don Tommaso."

⁓

That's another story. My father came from a wealthy family. He fell in love with my mother, but my mother's family had nothing. She was a beautiful person, but he married against the will of his father. His father didn't talk to him for awhile. My grandfather eventually helped my father and mother have a house...a house my father made bigger for his growing family. I respect my father. I was in Italy three years ago and somebody said to me, "Your father and mother gave you health." I didn't understand what he said. Was he talking about good genes? My father died at 92 and my mother was 95. There's no question they had good blood.

⁓

Anyway, when my father went to Rome, he found a job for Pasquale. The job was to work on the train, to go South and then to the North, and to work in the restaurant on the train. It was a First Class train. My father took him to meet the man who helped him get the job. In the front of the man, my brother-in-law said, "You want to give a job like this to me? I have an education," and things like that. Then he walked away. My father was embarrassed, but this man really liked my father. He said, "Don Tommaso don't worry too much. That's the way...one day this man is gonna find himself."

And one day he did find the job he wanted. He did it by himself, in his own field. I have a lot of respect, still have respect for him.

Anyway, one day Pasquale said to my father, "Why don't you send one of your sons to school? Why don't you send Ottavio to school?" And my father said, "I have five sons, all in cabinet work...I need their help." This is a true story, one of my sisters told me: he had four daughters before he had a son and he taught them to become cabinet makers because he needed help. My sisters worked in his shop. They learned how to nail things together. They really helped my father.

Going back now to my brother-in-law, who convinced me to go to school. I said, "Well, all right." Then he took me to another city, Avellino. It was half an hour away on the train from my town, Serino. He took me to talk to the principal of the school. The school was named the Instituto Commerciale. I put in my application, and then I went to this school. I did five years of school in Serino, and then I went to this school until I was 16. I was there four years. Everything worked out well. I passed all the tests. I was very good in school. The only thing was, my brothers all the time repeated in my house, "Why he gotta go to school and we gotta work?" It was bothering me, but I didn't listen.

I continued to go to school, and in the meantime, I was also a helper in the shop. When I came home from school, I used to help my father work. But my brothers still complained that they were working full time and I was just helping.

Every morning I used to get up early. I walked half an hour to get to the train, and then walked another half an hour to reach the school. I used to love the train ride with the kids, we were on the train about half an hour. It was very nice. One morning, when I was going to school, I had a fight with some of my friends. There was a girl who used to take the train with me, and these boys used to tease her. I had a big fight with them and came home with my nose all broken up. My father wanted to give me another beating because he said, "Why you...why did you start a problem?" My father was so good. In other words, he never got into fights. "You gotta try to not look for problems," he said. Anyway, there was no more trouble. I got in trouble trying to help this girl, but it worked out.

I loved the school and the teachers and they liked me. They would always ask me all the questions because I used to be the head of the class. In the end I passed all of the courses, I finished in four years. Then I was supposed to go another two years.

In the middle of the final two years, I had a little family fight. I was a little tired of hearing my brothers say, "What are you doing? We work, you do this..." I got up and said, "Stop! I made my decision!" When I reach a decision, it's very hard to come back. So, I finished with school and concentrated on working and making furniture.

"Look I want to learn," I said to my father. "I want to learn the things that you do, and I want to make expensive furniture. You remember, when you took me to Rome, you showed me all the furniture that you did for all those rich people. I want to do that. Do you want to show me?" My father was so excited. I concentrated on work and learned to build and to finish the furniture. I learned to do very high quality work. I am impressed with my father. Still now, I admire him. He was so good to guide us, but let us do what we felt like doing.

CHAPTER TWO

I Leave Serino to Learn My Trade Better

One day Benito, one of my friends, came over when I was working in my father's shop. He was visiting from Switzerland. He used to work for my father but moved to Switzerland because he could make more money. He invited me to go to Switzerland with him.

So, when I was 17 years old I went with him to Switzerland, to Lucerne, a beautiful city. They did not talk in Italian. They talked, I think, in French, French and German. The next day he introduced me to his boss. I saw a very nice-size shop. He used very fine wood, hard wood, oak, white oak, beautiful. He offered me a job, and in a few days, I became good friends with him because I gave him ideas. I made some sample pieces. Everything I put together he loved. And soon, he was offering me more money, but I never loved money. To me the money wasn't the most important thing. To me the most important thing was the connections, learning the trade, meeting people. That's what it was when I was young.

I'll never forget when one day he took me to his house and his wife said, "How old you are?" I didn't understand. She was talking a little Italian. She wanted a piece of furniture. In three days I made the piece of furniture she wanted, a roll-top desk of oak. She was very happy, and so was he.

The men in the shop used to say to me, "Why? You're crazy, you work so hard, they don't like us." But I believe in work, like my father taught me: "Respect people, do the work you gotta do, you gotta complete." I put furniture together so quickly, they really loved me. But I didn't like Switzerland too much, because you work so hard. You have to always work for a boss, you cannot open your own business. That's the idea I didn't like.

Before I went to Switzerland, I lived in our house. It was a five family house. One family that rented an apartment was a lady and her boy friend. They had a little boy. One of my sisters didn't want to give them the apartment because they had this illegitimate boy. But, my mother really liked her. Her boyfriend was an engineer. The company he worked for built a big road up the Monte Terminio in Serino. Anyway, she was a beautiful woman and I was young. I was probably too young for her.

But we become friendly, very friendly. I bring this up because, when I left, I didn't understand what she wanted. She was introducing me to her relatives. I didn't know what she had in mind, but my mind was clear. I was not looking for a problem. But I used to, you know, compliment her. That's the way I am. But her father thought we should be engaged. When I decided in Switzerland to go back home, my real worry was that when I went back I would see this lady. I did see her when I went home, but we ended our friendship.

I came back and I told my father I learned a lot and I had. And my father said, "Fine. Do whatever you want." Then I started building furniture the way they did in Switzerland.

It was beautiful. It was so beautiful, he said, "I am so excited." I tell my sons even now that when you work for yourself, you work hard. That's why when I went to work for this guy in Switzerland, I worked like I worked for my father. I didn't keep track of the time or things, just to complete the job.

Ottavio, age 18

I worked for my father for a while and everything worked out. My father was so happy, my brothers were happy and they saw new ideas. I'd taught them, showed them, how to build new furniture. One day I said, "Look, I gotta make a decision. I can't stay in this small town." I all the time looked for things to progress. So, I decided to go to Milano. It was the best thing that I did. I. told my father, "Look, I gonna go to Milano. I want to learn to make really good, good furniture." Milano was and still is the furniture capital of the world.

My idea was to look to the future. I could see there were five brothers all together, working with the family. In my head I said, "I gotta get out again and learn more." And then my father said that was the best thing to do. He said, "Milano is the key, with the best furniture in the world." So I made up my mind. I am the kind of person that, before I make up my mind, I ask myself ten times. Then, when I make a decision, that's it. Nobody could change my mind. That's the way I am...so far. So, I made some arrangements and I went to Milano.

As I said in the beginning, the whole key is the father. I used to ask my mother's advice about things and she would say, "Talk to Don Tommaso. Talk to him." I respect her because she loved my father and she respected the decisions that my father used to make.

Anyway, I took the train that went straight to Milano. I found a nice family and they let me stay with them. They had a very small shop in the town of Baruccano. Milano was about thirty miles away. Baruccano is a very small town, a beautiful place. It was all industrial. It was just what I was looking for. I used to keep all the time my eyes on women and fun things, but I promised myself that now, I would concentrate on learning as much as I could, without thinking about anything else. No joking around.

I had no money in my pocket. Then I got a little. Every week they used to pay me and I used to keep it. Then maybe sometimes I used to go out when everybody went out. I remember the people at the place where I worked. They'd go to a restaurant, and they would buy big meals, and I used to buy a little sandwich. I was very skinny then. I didn't eat a lot. Now I can eat for ten people.

I put it together. It was easier here than it was in Switzerland. Over here I said, "I can make a living". I loved the attitude, I loved the respect for people. When we use to go to a store or to a restaurant, people were polite, very nice.

⚭

One thing I am so proud of was all the education I got. I was able to talk to the people in Italy without making mistakes in words or grammar. The people in Milano liked me. I'll never forget this factory where I was working. Next door, there was another factory in competition with them. The people where I stayed didn't want me to talk to these people because they made the same kind of furniture.

Then, one day, I saw the wife of the competing factory owner yelling at this man. The man was so skinny! It was a Sunday and everybody had gone out. I was reading a book on the porch of the house where I was staying, and got up when I heard her. I said, "Look, I don't know why, but I hear you yelling. This makes my heart...." Later she told me the story, that the man was an alcoholic and he had a lot of problems.

25

In the meantime, she and I became friends. She was a nice woman, maybe 20 years older than me, but I would just talk to her. She was looking at me a lot of the time, but I was not interested in anything. I was interested in seeing her husband's shop.

One day she showed it to me. I went inside and met her husband, and when I told him where I was working, he said, "So, would you come here to work? I will give you more money." I said, "No, I can't do that." What I saw in his shop was some beautiful veneer work. When I left, I went home. It was Sunday and I spent half the day drawing what I'd seen in the five minutes I was in his shop. Then I went to a little convention in the town, a furniture convention...I showed the drawings. They said, "Who makes this?" I didn't tell, because I don't know... in business, particularly in the furniture business, you have to be so careful. I learned that in Milano. You can't show the things that somebody else did. It has to be something you created. But, anyway, I felt so good! This made me so excited! I wasn't looking for a good time.

But I was very young. One day my boss's son said, "Look my girlfriend has a sister, and we all want to go to this dance tonight". I remembered I didn't have good clothes, but he gave me some, so I went to the dance, it was good. Really, I had done so much. I was so busy learning. I was inside almost a couple of months, and didn't do anything fun, just concentrated on work. I had a good time that night.

In the meantime, I made a connection with a guy. This guy was the son of another big factory owner. Like I say, Baruccano is in North Italy, near Milano. It's called Brianza. Brianza is part of the Cantu. Between Como and Milano, there are all of these furniture makers. It's still now where I go. It's a lot of little factories and shops. Everybody used to make only one kind of furniture. One factory made a table, that's all they made, tables. Another one made end tables, another one headboards. It was good for me, when I met this guy, because he liked the girl I used to go out with, I said, "You take her, no problem." She was mad, but in the meantime, after work the next day, I went to see him.

In his small factory, I looked at the machines and concentrated on what they had. This way, I knew when I went back to my town and my father's little shop, I could show them how to build and what machines we needed to make better furniture.

I stayed in Baruccano, and I tried to work all around and discover things, but there were a lot of small factories. I used to knock on the doors and look inside at how they made furniture, but I had to do it very carefully, because these people didn't trust much. But the important thing was, I was learning, looking to fill up my ideas, to learn about the best furniture.

One day, at the place where I was working, the owners decided to go on vacation and invited me to go with them. We went to this place on Lago Maggiore. There was one island, I'll never forget, Isola Pescatore, where we ate. They ate in a better restaurant than I did. I ate in a smaller delicatessen because I didn't want to spend money. I tried to keep my money, to make sure I had it if I needed it. I was enjoying looking all around. I could see everyone was having a good time. I felt a little sad. Maybe because I was a little lonely... because, you know, far away from the relatives, all by myself.

I'll never forget sitting there on a little bench with a little old man. We had a nice conversation and I made him laugh. He wanted to know what I was doing over there. We had a good time talking. I thought, I hoped, that maybe someday I would come back to vacation in Lago Maggiore.

Anyway, when we returned and I started work again I knew that I had learned so much from living here in northern Italy. The people here were different than the people that I had grown up with in the south of Italy. I saw a big difference in this Milano region. I wasn't jealous in any way, but I learned. I saw these people, people who work hard and now had money, how they would spend money. To them having a good vacation, having fun was very important. On Monday morning when I started work after the vacation, I felt like singing in the shop. Everybody said, "Why are you so happy?" I had learned a lot on the short vacation. I learned so much in this Cantu, in this Brianza. There are 10-15 little towns filled with small shops, so on weekends after work, I used to go all around and visit them. That's why now it's so good for me when I go to Italy to do business. I had been there before.

One day, my boss called me up and said, "You got this special letter from your mother." I opened up the letter. It said I had to go back home because I had to go in the army. In Italy, at that time (1950's), they made you go in the army.

So I said goodbye to the people that I met, and thanks. I was very polite. The people liked me and they said, "Come back after the military. We will have a job for you. Our house is always open." It made me feel very, very comfortable to see all these people saying good-bye. And I'll never forget the lady next door. She really was pushing me to stay, "We'll give you a job." Maybe one day, they said, I could even be a partner in the business. But my goal was all the time to look for the future, to go back to Serino and build my own business, my own way, to be together with my family.

∽

Coming home was terrific. My mother...I missed my mother. She was a very small woman. I'll never forget, when I'd go away and when I'd come back, I'd pick her up in my arms. I'd swing her all around. She was so happy! She gave me a little special attention. I can understand. I think it's the old thing, some of my brothers used to be jealous, but the way I can figure it out is, when I was small I was sick, and maybe she couldn't forget that.

She loved everybody. She was so good and had no favorites. In other words, she had ten kids and I think she treated everybody the same. She was terrific. She and my father were wonderful. When I came home, I took a nice sleep. I slept for maybe 12 hours. In the morning, when I woke up, the first thing I did was go downstairs. We used to have the little shop next to the house. I said to my father, "Now I'll show you how to make furniture." I'll never forget, I started six bedrooms at one time. Everyone came to visit, I talked to all my friends and family. I missed everyone.

I remember there was all this excitement and I forgot about...I was so enthusiastic to talk about business... I forgot this letter that you gotta go in the army. Then, oh my God I read the letter and...all right! That is what I had to do. I think you had to serve for two years. We prepared the suitcase again. My mother was crying. My friends came and we had a big party in my house.

CHAPTER THREE

My Military Life

The next day I left to go to Cuneo. When I was in the army, I wrote every day in a diary about what I did. I gave it the title: "My Life in the Military."

2 May, 1956: Came back from Milano and left Serino. I left Serino and went to Cuneo. Cuneo is about 100 miles from Milano in Piemonte, Province of Torino. It's between the French Alps and Italy. In the train, I was sitting on a small seat and just looking around. I saw a lot of people who looked like they were going to the same place where I was going. I looked out the window. A lot of things were in my head, things like what am I going to find in this military life? Anyway, I was in Cuneo at 11:00 o'clock.

In the middle of Cuneo, I saw a very big street called Courso Nizza. There was a big piazza, with a big sculpture of Tocci Galemberte. It was called the Piazza Tocci Galemberte.

After that I visited the town San Rocco. The first thing in my mind, I said, "I want to have a nice dinner." Without thinking twice, I found this small trattoria. I went in and I ordered antipasto, fruit and the first course. I was very hungry from this big trip. The food was very good, and I ate really well. After I paid the bill and left this little trattoria, I was very, very happy. I looked at my watch. There was another 50 minutes before I had to go to the caserma, where they expected me to be present, to be in the army.

I was very strong. I think I walked all the way, over one mile, to go to the caserma. It was in a beautiful city. On my way I saw a beautiful store with a nice showroom of furniture.

As soon as I walked in the front of this big building, I saw one man standing motionless with a rifle in his hand. He was a Sentinela, in other words, a guard. He looked like a piece of sculpture. I was close enough to him to say hello, but you cannot talk to these guys. He just stood there...that's what they explained to me later. The second military man brought me inside and said the Sentinela was the symbol of the Caserma, the army base. Everything had to be straight, following orders. Then I was told to go inside through this door. I walked in. I was curious. This person was very curt: "Where do you come from?" Very mad. Very nasty.

I showed the paper I had in my pocket. I tried to be polite but he wasn't. He showed me another signpost. He started talking and then they gave me the destination where I had to go. This other man was a little funny. He took me where there were about 20 men, 20 soldiers like me. They were sitting on top of their suitcases. They looked very tired, like me. We came from every region in Italy. I was in the middle of them for about an hour. Then somebody came and we got into a truck.

In two kilometers, we reached another caserma. This was the company where I would be located, Fifth Company,

"Quinta Compagnia," they called it. When I walked into the office, I gave an officer all of my documents. After 10 minutes, they gave me two blankets and a couple of sheets.

I tried to be funny with the man who took me in, but this man was tough. He was very strict. He showed me a couple of pieces of metal. On this I had to make my bed. I tried to put everything together. I finally made the bed. At six o'clock in the morning, they started to scream like crazy. Everybody had to get up. I was so tired, it was very hard to wake up at six o'clock in the morning. I laugh now, but then it wasn't funny. This man, the one who was tough, was the caporale and the one who was going to instruct us.

Then we went for coffee. The coffee was funny. It was like brown paint. I thought, a professional painter could use it to paint a wall. And, at 12 o'clock, I can't describe what we ate. In my diary I wrote, "If I describe it I'm going to get indigestion."

Two days passed and I still had regular clothes. I told the caporale. Then they gave us some uniforms to put on. When I looked in the mirror, I looked like a Pulcinella. In other words, I looked very funny, all dressed in green. The maresciallo, the chief, who told us to put the uniforms on, was kind. He was one of the best, a sympathetic person. I liked him, and he liked me because I made him laugh. I remember the funny words he used, a vocabulary all his own, words he invented himself.

The next day they brought us to the barber, who cut off all my hair. With the uniform and no hair, I looked like somebody in jail. After the 14th day, they brought us to the infirmary. The infirmary was like an emergency room in a hospital.

They gave us a special needle, a very, very long needle that caused a lot of pain. This was so while we were in the army, we would get no infection. I saw a couple of people in front of me faint. After this needle, you had a fever for two days, a very high fever. This way they knew the effect of the medicine. It's good to know. That was the system in the army, anyway.

Then, for 20 days, we had to stay in the caserma, without going out. My new friends and I started to talk about what we were going to do when we could go out. We were going to go and see girls, there were a lot of things we wanted to do. We were young, but in the meantime, patient. Then we got very jealous because people started going out, people that came in after us. When they went out, they didn't look too good because the army coat was very long, all the way to the ground. My friends and I said, "If we gotta go out like that, we don't want to go out on the road."

But I decided to go out anyway. After 20 days, they gave us the O.K. to go out. We walked to the city. It certainly didn't look like it had when I came in. Anyway, I explored, I looked around...all around. I was feeling like a free man. But, whenever you saw people, every superior or army officer, you had to salute. Anyway, I went out a couple of times, but it was not fun. There were so many military in this city and the people, the girls at least, didn't seem to like the military.

One thing really made me so happy. We used to do a lot of training, running around. We used to, in other words, exercise early in the morning. It made the time fly and we felt stronger.

The head of my squad of 32 people was a caporale, who

came from Padua, in Northern Italy. He was very bad. I didn't like him. He made so much noise. Every night I was fighting with him to go out. He would then give me some penalty and say, "You can't go out tonight." Then he would send me to wash dishes. But I learned a lot. I learned not to talk back to people because if you did, they gave you a broom and told you to clean the street. That's true. My mother was right. Some people needed to go to the army and I was one of them.

Ottavio in the military

One night, I refused to clean a big pan in the kitchen and they put me in jail. They closed the door and I was all by myself. I slept on a piece of wood. That still didn't change me. But finally, one day, I decided to change. I learned to take orders and listen to them...to say, "Yessir!" when I didn't want to say, "Yessir!" That's the life of the young soldier. It was an experience.

I passed the course in 40 days and I did the Giuramento. The Giuramento is when you swear you will serve Italy in the army. Then they sent me to a special course to learn to be an instructor. They trained me to be an instructor for the new soldiers that came in, to prepare them to serve in the army.

The training was very hard because they treated us like animals. When you're an instructor, you have to do everything twice. Once for yourself and once to show the others how to do it. You have to show the soldiers how to shoot and how to jump on top of a wall. You teach them, you command people. I started to like being a boss. I remembered what my father said to me all the time, "You want to be boss! And now you got the job."

Anyway, I tried to have fun. I passed the course, one of the best. They gave me a paper to say I was good at jumping. I was really good. I remember when I was a Boy Scout there was a big wall in the church yard. I used to jump over this wall, back and forth all the time. I used to jump around like crazy. Anyway, they sent me to a special training camp, the name is San Rocco di Cuneo, to train people the way they taught me when I first came to the army. So, my job was to prepare men to be in the army, starting with very simple things...how they ate, the fork, the spoon, how they put socks on etc.

I'll never forget one guy. He came from a very small town, very country, a farm town. He said he never had socks on.

He had a toenail that looked like it was over one and a half inches long. I had to show him how you cut your toe nails. My job was to prepare them for army life. Then, you taught them how to march. I'll never forget one other guy, I don't remember his name now, but it was so funny. They punished me for what I did. You have to do: "Left, Right, Left, Right." When you say "Right" you push the right foot down to make a noise. He was always doing "Left, Right, Left, Right" and pushing the left foot down. So I put him on top of a little stool and I tied a string to his right arm, and I said, "Look, this is the right arm..." but the caporale saw me, "You can't do this! Make fun of people." Then he punished me. For one week I couldn't go out. That's the punishment they gave me.

But the soldier loved me because finally, he was marching right. It was embarrassing him to get it wrong.

I used to have fun, you know, being in charge for me was so good. The worst part was the time, during the course, that I fell down. They put a big ring in front of us, lit it on fire and you had to jump through it. When I showed this to my group, me, the instructor was supposed to do it first. I made a mistake, which was too bad. I fell. I was alright, but I wanted my team to win. I wanted my team to be the best. Anyway, we did not win.

Every 40 days, I used to train about 18-20 people. I did that for almost two years. You figure it out how many I trained. It was good. The caporale used to love it. The only thing he didn't like too much was when I pushed someone too hard. This was one part of my life, my army life.

Anyway, when I used to go out, I would prepare and fix my uniform nice. One night I went out with a friend of mine.

He said to me, "Ottavio, I gotta go someplace." I said, "Where are you going?" He said, "I gonna go to San Moritzio to a dance." I knew it was a nice place so I said, "O.K., let's go." We wore our uniforms.

We went in uniform, but the only people we could see dancing were the officers. They looked better, they had better uniforms. So my friend said to me, "Ottavio, I'm gonna call my sister and let her send us suits." And that's what he did.

So one night we went to the same place where these officers were. All of the women were over there to dance. The night was different because now we didn't have uniforms on. We met a couple of girls and danced. It turned out we had a good time.

I knew this guy, Gennaro, who could sing. And I pushed him to sing a song. What happened was, I went to the band and said, "Look I have a friend of mine, he sings, you wouldn't mind letting him sing a song?" They said that they didn't mind, and Oh, My God! He had a great voice, terrific...everybody clapped their hands, it was beautiful! He was shy, but I pushed him. Then I made believe I was singing. We had fun! We were supposed to be in the caserma by 12 o'clock - midnight. If you were half an hour late, you would be punished.

We were still there at one o'clock. Then we saw the colonel of the caserma. We saw him with a woman, maybe his wife, I don't know. He said, "What are you doing here?" We made believe we didn't know him. When my friend and I got back, we got punished. They put us in jail for ten nights. During the day you had to do your work, but at night you took your blanket and you stayed in this room. It wasn't really that tough.

It wasn't such a big thing. We did have a good night, it was a nice dance. My friend and I became very strong friends. It's very nice to meet and make friends in the army.

So now, I needed to make a little money. My friend said, "Ottavio, we don't have any money. How are we going to go to this place again?" The government pay was very little, just enough to buy maybe a pack of cigarettes.

I got to know the colonel who is above the maresciolo in the caserma. I used to go to his house and polish some of his furniture. I'd go on Sundays. The colonel's daughter was there when I would go. She was helping me. We became good friends.

Then I started to make a few bucks. There also was an antique store in town. I'll never forget. I stopped in because furniture is in my blood. I asked if they had any work. The guy said, "Well, can you fix this one little table?" I fixed the table and he gave me in exchange a gift certificate to go eat dinner.

My life is so good sometimes. It's as if somebody guides me because the gift certificate he gave me was for the same trattoria I went to when I first came to Cuneo. I loved the food there. It reminded me of my mother's cooking. It was a very good experience.

In the meantime, when my father wrote to me, he asked me why I never asked for money. My father had been in the army and knew about the low pay. I told him that I was doing some work. He told me that he use to do the same thing.

My father was a cabinet maker and a builder of furniture, so when he was in the army, during WWII, his main job was to be in contact with the officers because he was in the Corpo di Finanza, dealing with taxes. He got to know the officers well. So, he did work for them too.

One day on a short break I went to Parma with one of my friends. He wanted to introduce me to his family. It was near Parma, where they make the parmigiano cheese. (They make both the parmigiano cheese and prosciutto there.) I love both the cheese and the prosciutto. They make prosciutto from the pigs which are fed the same milk which is used to make parmigiano cheese. Its amazing.

My next break was when I went back to Serino because my mother didn't feel good. She sent the army a letter saying that I had to go home. When I got back home, she was O.K.

While I was home, I met a girl who, with her father, was visiting from the United States. They were visiting a neighbor. Anyway, the girl and I went out for a short time. She went back to America and she wrote to me. Her and her father invited me to come to America. Her father said if you come to America, you know how much money you'll make. But, anyway, this was in the middle of my life in the army and I had to go back to the army.

I want to describe the caserma. In front of the caserma was the courtyard with a small tree. We would do our drills there every day, and I would always look at this tree. The reason I mention the tree outside the caserma is because it was so beautiful. I was lucky enough, after 40 years to go back and visit Cuneo. I went back to the caserma and saw the tree. It had grown to about 75 feet high. It was a pine tree. I picked up a pine cone and brought it home with me.

One time I had an appointment to go finish a bedroom set. The customer was supposed to give me, I think, $200.00. I worked on the set for two weeks and it was almost finished. And then I couldn't go out.

I was restricted in the caserma. I went to the maresciallo and said, "Look, I gotta go." They wouldn't let me go. But, anyway, during the night...early in the morning...I jumped over the wall and went. I did my job and then I came back. I finished this beautiful bedroom set. The people paid me, they were so happy. But, the maresciallo found out I had gone. So I got punished again. Another ten days in jail.

When my military life was almost over I went back again to Serino. I went back a week before I finished the military and tried to prepare my territory, to see, when I came back, where I was I going to make furniture. I talked to my brothers, things like that. Anyway, I started a few jobs and then I went back to the army to finish up my duty.

We had a big function. I'll never forget the people I did work for when in the army...the captain, the colonel, and their family all came and brought me presents. Everybody was happy. They gave all of us a diploma. The people were wonderful, but it's really sad when you leave all your friends. Friends you know you will miss because you had spent so much time together and you really knew them well. To me friends are really important. That's my character, to meet people and know the right people. You never know when you need a friend, plus it's beautiful. I don't know how to describe it. Friendship is very important.

CHAPTER FOUR

I Return to Serino

When I was discharged from the army, I felt so good. My mother was so happy. My mother cleaned my uniform, the green uniform with the red tie. Red tie because I was near the Alps. The Garibaldine Regiment they called it, stationed in the Alpini Mountains. When I came back home, my mother and my sisters prepared regular clothes for me. They were really nice. My mother used to prepare so much food, but I wasn't use to eating a lot. To me food was not important. I was so skinny because I never ate, and I still jumped around.

Coming home, I started a new life in our small town. I started work. I told my father, like I said in the beginning, my father and I used to talk, and then I talked to my brothers. I said, "Look, I am in charge." And we bought a new machine, the machine I saw in Milano, the one to finish furniture. We did well, nothing big, but nice. It used to be, like over here, people came to you, you did a job for them, you got paid.

One day one of my friends came and said, "You gotta be my best man in my wedding." This was the first of many weddings that I was asked to be best man. I used to buy a lot of wedding rings. The custom in Italy is that the best man always buys the wedding rings for the couple. I'll never forget the jewelry guy (maybe that is why I love gold so much). He had a jewelry store in the Sala, part of Serino. I used to buy the rings there. He and I became good friends. And then the new couples always bought our furniture. Sometimes I used to charge a little bit more to pay for the rings, but they loved me. That's why when I go to Italy now I still have so many friends. They miss me, and I miss them. Then I decided to open a store in the Sala, besides the one we had in another section of the town.

We did very well. Everybody earned money. We gave it to my father. Everything was in the family. I know now that that was the wrong way to do it, but this was the way the system was over there. It's very hard to understand the culture in the smaller town, the family is so close. But one thing I know, my father used to say he was very lucky, ten kids and all ten got married. My sisters all married beautiful men, very nice. The grandchildren, my father used to say, "Look how beautiful!" They were beautiful. He was very lucky.

೮ youa

My brothers-in-law all had nice positions. One was a police commissioner. He and my sister have three girls and one boy, four kids. He's the only one in my family with four kids. The others have one or two or three. They never became like my father. My father used to tease everybody when we used to be together. He'd say, "What happen? Look at this. Everybody has one, two. I'm the only one with 10." I'll never forget one time, when I was visiting from the United

States, and we were all at the table, I asked, "But how did you do it? You made Momma happy all the time!?" I used to joke around with my parents. He loved me. He was my friend. That's why I loved him so much. I learned to handle things in a different way, to never make him mad. I never...I swear I never made my mother mad, but with my father I might have said some words. He watched me grow in a lot of ways. He knew I had the business clear in my brains. Then, when I came back from Milano, I tried to do things like I had learned. He let me do it. He said, "Go." It was O.K. He was... anyway, it was amazing.

My first sister, Assunta, the one who married the police commissioner is named after my mother. She came to the U.S. to visit me after her husband died. The next one is Luisa. Luisa told me the story of how her husband, Alfredo, came to ask my father for her hand. That's the way it was 60 years ago. He went to my father and said, "I want to go out with your daughter." My father said, "What do you do for a living?" He said, "The only thing I do... look, I took these with me."

He had tools, he was a brick layer. He took the trowel, the one you use to put the cement on the wall with. He said "That's what I have." My father gave the O.K. He saw he was a hard-working man. He went out and made a very good living. They had two kids. He's dead now; that's the second brother-in-law dead. What are you going to do? My sisters are getting old. One is now 80 years old. Another is 78.

My sister, Luisa, was very conservative, like my mother. When my father was working, he made money and gave it to my mother. My sister did the same thing. I'll never forget, my father said, "I give $100.00 to your mother and I find...

about a month later, I find $100.00." I'd say, "How did she feed us?" My sister Luisa also could save money. Alfredo became a very big builder. First he started fixing old houses then, he started building houses. He once built a church. In other words, this Alfredo, after he was married about 20 years, had the feast of a millionaire. This is what they do in Italy when they are successful. I heard about it from the family. He had a son, an architect, and a daughter. That's where I stay now when I go to Italy.

I started to work, eventually looking into the city to get better jobs, to be in touch with people who had more money, like doctors and things like this, but still working with my father and family. I used to build big wall units. And things worked out all right.

One day, I decided to buy a car. I bought a little Alfa Romeo. It was good, but I had to share it with my brothers. Whoever got up first in the morning used it. The same thing went for clothes. I'll never forget one of my brothers, Ennio, used to go out with this girl...now they are married. She gave him for his birthday a beautiful shirt, a red shirt. I love red, that's my favorite color. One day I was supposed to go out with some girl. With the new car, things like this, I wore the red shirt. His girlfriend saw me. The next day, my brother took the shirt from me and tore it up. He put it under his feet. He said, "You can't do this!" It wasn't funny, but this is true. We had an argument. Then we hugged and laughed. We still talk about it all the time.

Every day we worked till five o'clock. Then we used to get out of the shop and go out. Sometimes we used to go into the city. This was the life over there. In the smaller town, we used to stay near the bar. You went to the bar to have a few cups of coffee and meet your friends. We played card games and that was it. Outside people were walking back and forth, "passegiate" they call it.

My brother Paolo and I started to build a mill. We bought a tractor and cut down trees. It was a mistake to do this mill because we should have concentrated on furniture and doors and other big things. My father wanted to get a little bigger, because there were five brothers, but the mill was a mistake. Anyway, we made money but we worked too hard.

One time, as I went to cut this tree using the tractor, I almost died. The tractor turned over.

We had a big saw on the back of the tractor, and when we moved down the hill, the saw came over us. We dove to get out of the way. It was a miracle that we didn't get hurt. The tractor landed almost on top of me. It was terrible!

But, we cut a lot of trees. First we'd cut trees to use for ourselves. Other times we cut trees for other people and we would charge them. It was a little different this kind of business for us, but in smaller towns years ago, nobody else had this kind of machine. I spent six or seven years doing this.

☙

Then I started going out with this woman. She was a good businesswoman and she thought I wasn't concentrating the right way on business things. She used to have a big business with her mother. I think the father had died. She wanted to move her business out from Serino. She said, "Ottavio, you should do this too...build your own business." She wanted to help me grow my own business, not let the family business grow. They had a big business selling beer and soda. I often brought her to my house. My mother liked her, my father loved her because, all the time she came to visit me, she brought a case of beer for him. He loved her! And he knew she had a lot of money, but I wasn't interested in these things. One day she did move to another city, bought land, built her business and we went separate ways.

In one way she was right, I can see it now; she was smart. This woman was very, very smart. I give her a lot of credit, a lot of respect. I give it to my wife, too. If it weren't for Anna, I don't think I would be in the place I am now, because woman have a different view in general. They look at things differently. They're very...I don't know, I don't want to get too deep in this, but I have a lot of respect for woman.

Anyway, how I met this woman was very interesting.

One day I was going into Avellino. I was going in to buy some lumber. I saw this guy standing on the street corner. He wanted me to give him a ride. This didn't scare me. Years ago it was different, especially in that area. There was no crime. So, I gave him a ride. His name was Aldo. As we came into his small town, he said, "I want you to meet my mother." So I went in. She was a beautiful woman. We all talked. She didn't know me, but she put food on the table. We became good friends.

Aldo's father was a politician, a lawyer. He had a lot of power in Italy, especially in the city of Avellino. Aldo himself is now a City Counselor and President of the Avellino Workers Compensation. We are still friends. Anyways, after dinner, Aldo's sister introduced me to this woman who then invited us to her home. We were all friends for quite awhile.

❦

Now I know a little bit of life. Marriage is very beautiful. It's hard to describe. It's beautiful to have a companion. That's the best thing, to have someone you trust, someone to understand you. That's why I put marriage on a pedestal. I became very serious when I married my wife over here. I'll discuss it more later. It's a little confusing to talk about it, but the key is to catch the right person, to have a nice family. That's a little bit complicated, that's a bit hard, but that's why I admire my father.

My fourth sister, Filomena, is another story. She was a little bit unhappy when she got married because some of my brothers and sisters didn't go to the wedding. I didn't go either. It's a long story.

Her boyfriend was our neighbor, but he was a little older than my sister and had been married before. His wife had died in an accident. Everyone said he was too old for her. I liked my future brother-in-law, but you respect the decision of the older brothers, and follow their steps. So, we didn't go to the wedding. She married him and they had a beautiful son. He was a hard working man. He did very well. He was a gunsmith and he made good money. He led a very simple life. He came to the United States for a visit and there's a funny story about him.

When I took him into New York City, we went to the Empire State Building. At night, we went to a nightclub where there was a dancer. I gave her some money so she would dance for him. He was a little nervous, but laughed all night. When he went home to Italy he told his wife, my sister, the story. She laughed and thought it was so funny.

Then there is my youngest sister, Franca. She's a very special person. I want people to know a little bit of what my sister is like. She took on the full responsibility of my mother and my father in their later years. I was going to Italy so many times to see them, and I saw how she took care of them in their house. She moved with her family into an apartment in their house. I'll never forget how she took care of my father, and then my mother. It's amazing what she did.

Through all those years, she raised three kids. Her husband is terrific. God gave my parents a gift, what she did. That's my belief because sometimes they put older people in a convalescent home, but she spent time with my mother and my father, plus raised a family. In the meantime, they all lived in my father's house, which he liked. It worked out well because she got a part of the house in the end.

One time, when I went to visit my mother, Franca said, "Ottavio, I do this because of my heart, not for anything else; because I love my mother and father." You could see it by the look in her eyes, her expression. You could see there was love...she did it with a real heart... and I am very proud of her. She's a special girl, my little sister. It's beautiful talking about her.

I love my family. I'm so proud of my father and my mother. What it took to raise ten kids! To have a lot of sisters, a lot of brothers, is something special. Sometimes it is very complicated. I think sometimes that I am the guy that caused a little trouble by going to Milano and Switzerland, but I loved all the people I met and the experience I had. Things worked out.

When I went back to Serino, I had a wonderful time at first.

I loved what I was doing, working in the family business. The best part was my father working with us and making furniture. He knew so many things. But, Serino was a small town. I used to go to Naples a lot, I loved that city. Naples had a lot of big buildings, and the people that lived there wanted special furniture.

Once I bid out a company, bigger than me, to build a wall unit in Naples. The job was pretty big. When I told them the price, I had charged 150,000 lire more than the other people. They told me it was too high, could I do it for less. I refused. The owner of the complex said "You gotta be good because how can you refuse a job like this for a lousy 150,000 lire." He wanted to bargain with me. I said "No, there is no question. That's it. I did my figures, you want my work?" I did get the job.

I then met the architect for the complex, a woman architect. She loved the work that I did. We spent a lot of time there, and the work came out so good. When it was finished it was in the newspaper, but she used her own name. O.K.I got my money. I wasn't interested in publicity then. Now I understand what it means. I was only interested in my father's business. He was the key, what he created. I all the time put him as number one. We were all second, in other words.

My father was proud of me. I'll never forget, after we finished this job, he took me to this big church. They wanted some special work done. When my father took me there, the nuns wanted to deal with me, but I said, "No, no, my father is the key. I learned from him." He was...Oh, I loved him! He said, "Ottavio, you can do it, don't worry about me, don't worry about it. That's O.K." I can still see him, when he put his arm on top of my shoulder. They wanted me. How am I going to do this? He said "No worry, the most important, you get the money and this way we have a few more lire...." In other words, you know, we could buy a new machine.

It was wonderful. Now I understand. It was like the father gave a chance to the son, and the son could... I didn't want to take advantage of anything. I can see now, my sons work with me. John and Thomas are so terrific. They are good kids, you see ... they are very respectful. My wife taught them to respect. That's most important. I know, I learned that from my parents. Respect people. "Don't be rude," my father always said. I learned so much from him.

CHAPTER FIVE

I Leave for the United States

Like I said, I was looking all the time to move ahead. I saw there wasn't enough room in the business with my brothers. So, in 1966, I made my decision to come to the United States. I went to talk to my father and he said, "Ottavio, do whatever you want." Then I talked to my brothers. Anyway, it worked out. I was young. I'll never forget, when I told my mother she started to cry. I put all my ideas together and said, "I gotta go." But, when I went to get the ticket, the guy at the passport office said, "Ottavio, I don't think you can go. You gotta go as a tourist. To immigrate, you need money, and you don't have enough money in the bank to go." Years ago, to immigrate to the United States was very complicated.

So I went to talk to my sister Luisa, the one whose husband was a contractor. I told her I didn't have enough money in my bank account to immigrate to the U.S. I had just enough money to buy my ticket. But, I said, "If you put money in my account, I can get authorization to get the ticket." That was the situation. You had to show you had enough money in the bank. I worked on my sister and she said, "Look, I'll give it to you, but on Monday morning you have to bring it back because my husband has to make a big deposit on a job." I said, "Don't worry." That's what I did. I took the money to the bank. The bank gave me a receipt, and then I went to the travel agency. They told me, "You're all set, but the only thing is you have to go First Class."

In April, 1966, I left for the United States. I took a boat called the Queen Anna Maria. It was a beautiful boat, a Greek line. It left from Naples. I packed my suitcase and then my friends, my six good friends, took me to Naples. We went to a restaurant and I almost missed my boat because, as we were saying our good-byes, we started drinking and this and this. But, anyway, I did get on the boat.

On the boat, I remember very clearly, when I got to my room there was a beautiful desk and there was an invitation. I was invited to have dinner with the captain of the boat. They treated people a little better in First Class. And this is funny now. When I had dinner at the captain's table, they served lobster. Believe it or not, I'd had never had a lobster in all my life. I was so impressed because they served the lobster with cognac on top. The lobster was all afire when they put it on the table. I didn't know how to eat it. I was thinking maybe I should eat the whole shell. I watched the other people and how they started to crack it. Sitting next to me was the captain's secretary. She showed me how to eat it. She and I became good friends. She kept me company the whole trip from Naples to New York.

Ottavio in first class with the Captain
on the Queen Anna Maria 1966

This trip was so exciting. It took a long time to come over here. Every night I sat in the middle of these aristocratic people. I had to dress up every night. So, after a while, what I did was I moved into the Second Class. I went over there and met some people. It was a little different. Everybody talked Greek because it was a Greek boat. The food was terrific. I had a really good time. But then, I kept thinking I didn't know what I would find in the United States. I was taking a big chance leaving Italy.

I will always remember all the good times on the boat. It was a great experience! You saw families...I'll never forget there was a family with three kids. They were moving. I don't know what they were, whether they were Greek or not. They sat at my table every night. They were so professional. I saw love from the mother, the father and the kids. It was really nice.

I love to dance. I was young and I had no pain. I learned Greek dancing. I'll never forget this man...we sat at the bar and started to drink. He told me he was going to Canada. I said, "What are you going to Canada for?" He said, "I go for work." Then he said, "Where are you going?" I told him "I am going to the United States. I gotta just take a chance and see what happens. Who knows?" We became friends. I forget his name now. I don't remember how many days we took from Naples...maybe eight or nine days. I don't remember.

We stopped at Halifax. I went out with my new friends. We visited this church, such a beautiful church, but in the meantime, we almost missed the boat. Oh, my God! It was so scary!

We also had a stopped in Portugal. I saw this big sculpture of Christopher Columbus. We got off the ship. We had about three or four hours there. I went with my friends to eat. We ate sardines. They have the freshest sardines in Portugal! I think that's why I love sardines. Really they have good fresh fish. And then, finally, we came to New York.

CHAPTER SIX

Beginning a New Life in the United States

When I arrived I stayed in New Rochelle, New York. My brother, Paolo, was already here. It was...really, in the beginning, it was very tough. But, I started to learn, in my own way. I missed the rest of my family. I missed what I'd left.

When I was first came over here, I started to get a little lazy because I wasn't doing anything. I talked to a few Italian friends, but I didn't speak English. You know its a really different language from Italian. One Sunday I went by myself into New York City. What impressed me so much was the smoke that came from the street. I thought maybe it was the subway, but now I know they have smoke that comes down from all those big buildings. I spent a lot of time going by myself into New York City because New Rochelle was a much smaller city. I started to fall in love with New York City.

I walked up and down all the streets, I'll never forget, I passed this big church (I know now it was St. Patrick's

Cathedral). I went in and prayed for my mother, things like this. I was starting to get homesick, I really missed her, and this was after only a few weeks.

I found a part-time job making furniture in New Rochelle, but then I saw they took advantage of me. It's a long story. I don't want to mention what I went through because it's sad. They paid me $1.00 an hour. They used to make a lot of money on top of me. In the meantime, I started to get the feeling that this wasn't the kind of work that I wanted to do, building closets, things like this. I tried to make a decision. It was so hard.

One day I met some people. I went into New York City with them and I found a job there. That was the most important thing for me. Now, I knew I could not joke around, I just had to sell myself.

So in September of 1966, I started to work at the Longines Wittnauer Watch Company on Fifth Avenue. They gave me very little money, about three dollars an hour to do maintenance work. I liked the place, but it was tough. I was not making much money, and I spoke no English. I'll never forget going to buy lunch. I found a delicatessen. One lunch I remember cost so much money...seven or six dollars, something like this.

It's a little sad now...but I slept in this small hotel on Sixth Avenue. You paid by the night. I can't describe how bad it looked, but that was all I could afford. Anyway, I worked and worked.

One day I went and talked to the boss. There was an Italian guy with him. He became a translator for me. My boss really liked me, and he wanted to help me. I was lucky because they had another store on Madison Avenue, Tourneau Jewelry, a very big store where they sold the expensive Longines watches. Around four o'clock that day, he said, "My brother has some work for you over there." So then I went to work there after 5 o'clock every day. I stayed until ten o'clock in the night.

And the money I made for the night work was more than I made in the day at Longines. Then I started to get a feel for the dollar, but I still didn't make a decision if I wanted to stay in the U.S. I'll never forget, my father and my mother said, "Well look, if you really don't like it, come back. Forget about it. You have things over here."

But I liked the big city. I enjoyed it because I found the city full of life, plus I liked the people I met at my work, particularly my boss, Harry Kerben. He really got to know me. The Italian guy, my translator, told him "Ottavio doesn't really do this kind of work. Ottavio makes furniture." Then he took me to his house.

So working in the Longines Watch Company I did maintenance work, but I didn't care. I took everything I could get.

At the Longines, I started to put in dropped ceilings, things I had never done in my life, but it was good because I was learning new things and I liked working with my foreman. I'll never forget him. He was an older man. His name was Carl Freedman. He came from Germany. He tried to talk to me, but he didn't speak one word in Italian. He spoke German and English. But, anyway, he was terrific. One day at lunch time, when we sat down, he saw me with a can of tuna. I love tuna, canned tuna. Still now I go crazy for it. I went into this delicatessen and bought it. When I was ready to open the can, he said, "Come with me. You made a mistake. That's not for you." We went back to the deli and he tried to explain that it was food canned for a cat. I didn't know…there was no picture on it!

He started to like me because I worked very hard. He was most grateful because the jobs that he gave to me were the ones that the boss had given to him. I was young. Climbing up and down, things like this. He was happy because he said to me he never had a helper. You know, my father trained me this way, to always work hard.

So, every day I worked at the Longines. They gave me I remember maybe $100 a week. Then I would go to work at the store on Madison Avenue until ten o'clock. And then on Saturdays and Sundays, I used to go to my boss's house and build some closets. That was a very good connection. He was nice, but he didn't pay me a lot. He gave me presents. He gave me some clothes. I didn't care. I didn't need clothes, but I took them because the man was so nice.

Working with Carl, now that's the key. One day he took me to a bank. He said, "Look, you gotta open an account in the Bank of New York on Fifth Avenue. He taught me how to save. "I don't care," he said, "Even if you put in ten dollars a week. This is the way in America. You gotta save." I respected him. I learned so much from him.

One day, he sat down and he put his feet up…it was at lunch time…and he said, "You gotta learn one word a day. "Hammer, nails,screws…." And he really worked with me, but then it was funny, because my boss one day said, "Ottavio, you talk like a German." But I kept trying. I worked hard and in two or three months I saved about $300.00-$500.00, and I was learning English. I had some Italian lire left, I put it in an envelope, $40 maybe, I don't know. I sent the money to my mother. That's how I started my life in America.

ᘒ

I was so excited being in New York City by myself. But then I realized I was paying too much for the hotel. Also, the people who lived there would make so much noise. The district was bad. In the meantime, I was looking to save money. I worked all day and at night I just wanted to have a place to sleep.

One day I asked Carl "What is this?" I had killed a bug and put it in a piece of paper. I said, "This kind of bug is in the bed, and when I'm sleeping they bite ...what are they?" "He said, "This is a roach." He understood my problem. He said, "Oh, my God. Maybe we should find you a better place to live." He talked to some watchmaker and asked him if he could find a place for me to live.

When I first came, I was living in New Rochelle, and then I went to New York City. Now this guy took me to his house in New Jersey, but it was too much to travel. He found me another place, but it was too much money. They wanted me to rent an apartment. I said, "I don't want an apartment," but I stayed there maybe two or three months. Then I rented a little room in the basement. Meantime, I started making money and putting the money in the bank.

My boss was excited about the workbench I was making for the watchmakers. When I studied in Switzerland, I learned things that helped me create this bench. When I made the first one he was so happy. Then I made more. I also started to put up wallpaper. This created a whole new look for the company. I had never put up wallpaper in my life, but Carl showed me how. Mr. Kerben was so excited because it made the place look so much better. I never asked for more money because they were going to sponsor me. I paid my taxes. I don't know how the system worked, but they needed papers for immigration.

Mr. Kerben then introduced me to this lawyer who brought me to the immigration office. He was a very nice lawyer, very nice in the beginning, but what happened is another story.

I was making furniture for Mr. Kerben's wife. She was so nice. I made a beautiful cabinet for her for her house. I made a nice connection. I was all by myself. I didn't want to be involved with friends, I just concentrated on work. I'll never forget, one day, I started to do some part time work for some people I met at the Longines. They soon said, "Why don't you leave the Longines and work the whole week on your own? You do such good work." I said, "No, I can't." I didn't want to leave the Longines because I was looking out for my papers to stay in this country and the Longines was helping me.

Longines is famous not only for its watches but also for its Atmos clock. The clock's case is made in brass. My boss said, "Can you create something in wood?" So he let me work at night in the shop. I bought a few little machines and I created this wooden Atmos clock. It took time, but they liked it. And he started to like me even more. He told the immigration lawyer: "We need this man." They took this Atmos clock, they let me make two, and they brought one to Switzerland. In Switzerland they made ten thousand of them. I was so happy the day they gave me a present of one of the wooden Atmos clock. I still have it in my house.

Now, I was young, and I was missing my friends and my family. I called Italy, I wrote to everyone in Italy, but what kept me going was concentrating on work and keeping busy. I started to have a little pain in one leg. I was putting in a drop ceiling in the building, it was a big space, maybe a thousand square feet. I had to be on top of the ladder all by myself. So I found some friends from New Rochelle to come work with me for the Longines. They came to the city, and then I had three men working for me.

But now there was a little problem. My boss said he wanted to talk to me. One day, he came into the shop, it was eight o'clock at night. Carl had left. He used to leave about five o'clock. I stayed till eleven o'clock. Mr. Kerben was so good to me. He saw me work late so he would let me stay in the shop. So sometime, instead of going to the hotel, I would sleep in the shop. I would put down a piece of plywood and sleep on it. In the morning I just got up. Nobody knew but the boss. I had the key. I was in control of the shop. I had a little stove. I used to make a little soup. This helped me to save money, but I'll never forget my mother writing, "Please eat!" Things like this. She was so cute. Then I found this Greek restaurant on Forty-Eighth Street, and every couple of days, I used to go over there. I'd have spaghetti and they'd put a steak on top of it. This was a big meal for me. It would last me all day. I really enjoyed it.

After about a year working there, my boss gave me the O.K. to build furniture in the company shop on my own time. Mr. Kerben was a kind man.

I'll never forget this woman, Rita. She said, "Ottavio, I need a television stand." So, I made it for her. She was so nice. She came with her car to pick it up. She paid me $500.00 or $600.00, I don't remember. I went straight to the bank. This was my first customer.

Carl taught me to save. I have so much respect for him. Now, as I said before, my boss came in to talk to me. He said, "Look, we decided to do something." I tried to understand, but I could tell by his eyes that he was very serious. He didn't want to talk to me in the front of anyone, because sometimes I used to call the man to translate. But I understood that he wanted to talk privately.

Anyway, he talked to me and said, "Look, we've decided, since you have to tell Carl what to do, you should be the foreman." I said, "Look, I can't do that..." Then, he realized, he understood me. "No, I will never go against this man. This man is so nice to me, he is a good man." Because he was starting to get old, they tried to get rid of him. Give me his job. The next day I said to Carl, " I'm never gonna do this to you."

I had already started to make some connections, I had a few jobs. The owner of this other building, on 58 Fifth Street, wanted to hire me. Someone told him about me. He tried to get me to take the job, but my idea wasn't to be a maintenance man for long. My job was a cabinet maker, a furniture maker. Every day, when I was working for the Longines Company, at lunchtime I used to go look at furniture. I used to go to see new things. I hoped that maybe one day I could have a business, but in the meantime, I was in the city doing all kinds of work.

One day, this man who owned the building on 58th Street took me into his office. You should see the office he had! But anyway, I did some work for him. He paid very little, very, very little. Carl said to me, "The work that you did for him may be worth around $5,000.00." I did it for $700.00. Then one day...one day he gave me two steaks. What was I going to do with two steaks? I was sleeping in the shop. I put them on top of the refrigerator where I kept my lunch. I took a piece of metal that I found in the garbage. I cleaned it up. I put it on top of the stove. (There was a small stove to heat the glue for making cabinets.) I put the steaks on top, cooked them, and then I ate them with a knife. This way I saved money. But, in the meantime, I couldn't believe somebody would give you steaks. Everything was new, but everything was good.

My boss then hired two Jamaican men to work with me, Louie and Jimmy. They used to go out every night to buy dinner and they would buy it for me too. They brought me all different kinds of Jamaican food. Now I had more friends. In the meantime, Carl showed me another trick about money. One day, he said to me, "Ottavio, you're putting too much money in the bank." He was like my father, such a nice guy. Then he told me about stock. In Italy I never heard about stock. When I was talking to my Italian friend, the one who used to do the translation for me, he said, "Oh, Ottavio, I have a broker." Then he gave me the name. I'll never forget the first one I bought, Con Edison Utility. I spent maybe $200.00...$300.00. The key was to try to make my money grow, to save more money. My idea was the future.

On Friday nights I used to go to school to learn English. I

was thinking, I want to get a drivers license. I had to take the test. When you want something, you do what you have to do. Anyway, I learned a little bit.

⁕

One day I met this watchmaker, Simon Kornbluth. He heard from my boss, Harry Kerben, that they trusted me and that they left me in charge in the building. There were watches all around the place, and they knew I wouldn't steal anything. One day Simon said, "In my house I have a basement that I would like to finish." He also wanted some cabinets built. So one Friday he took me with him on the train. We went from New York City to Canarsie, in Brooklyn.

This is another good thing that happened in my life. He was a very nice man, very nice. Simon also introduced me to his Italian neighbor. He too wanted to fix his basement with build in cabinets. So, on Saturday, I worked in his friend's basement. I put paneling in the basement and started to build the cabinets. When it was five o'clock, I said, "Look, I gotta leave." I was living in New Rochelle then and it would take about 2 hours to get home. He said, "Why you gonna go to New Rochelle now? Why don't you stay over here, sleep in the basement?" So I did, and the next day I worked in Simon's house. Simon asked me "Where did you sleep?" I told him and he said, "No, no, no. You can't sleep in the basement." Simon had two daughters, he said he would give me one of his daughters room to sleep in.

Now I had to find an excuse with the other man. I didn't want to make the Italian man feel that I did not want to sleep over there anymore, but I wanted to stay at Simon's house. I told him I was going to work at Simon's house till one o'clock in the morning, and then the next morning I was going to take the train with him to go to work. I'll never forget Simon's wife, Trudy. She was deaf, but her and I could understand each other. She also was a wonderful woman and a very good cook. She would cook dinner, and then make me eat at the table with the family. I appreciated it so much, to see something like this. I hadn't had a really good family dinner in a long time.

At the Longines, I used to work from six o'clock in the morning to one o'clock in the night. Imagine how much money in overtime! Sometimes, I put together maybe $400.00 in overtime a week. It was a lot of money then. I loved it and little by little I forgot about Italy. I forgot about everything because I was concentrating on my future and my ideas. One day, on Eighth Avenue, I looked at a little shop. They had a couple of cabinets they wanted to refinish. The guy wanted to hire me. I said, "Forget it." But that was my goal, maybe one day I would open my own store.

My boss was so attached to me because I was doing such good work, making these watchmaker benches and fixing up the offices. Then one day we heard that they were bought by another company. Westinghouse bought Longines and I was now working for them. I also now had three men working for me. But then, one day, my leg really started bothering me.

I accumulated good money, maybe I reached $10,000.00. I was feeling like a millionaire. I thought look what I did, only with my hands, things like that. I used to go to the bank every week. They used to give you a little bank book. Carl was worried. He said, "Banks can go broke. You have to go to another one." I said, "What are you talking about?" He explained it to me, so I went to another bank. Now I had two bank books. Carl worked hard all his life. He lived in an apartment in New York with his wife and two kids. One day, Carl...he was so good to me... he took me to his weekend house in Milford, Connecticut.

His wife was so nice. Really, she was also German. She tried to tell me "You gotta marry a German girl." I didn't understand and I said, "Carl, what is she talking about?" Carl laughed, but he too thought I should have a girlfriend. Forget about a girl, I was not attached. I was attached to making money. My thing was just to work, just to concentrate on work.

Then one night after work I took a train from New York City to New Rochelle, and I met this girl on the train. She was very nice and we started talking. She brought me one Sunday to a museum. When I was there I was thinking, why am I in this museum? I lost about $200.00...because that's what I would have made in one day if I had worked. It was nice. I had a good time but...

Back now to the new Longines, the new boss, the big officer from the Westinghouse Company, wanted new wood panels on the walls, new desks and things like this. I got three more men to help, and I was working with them into the night. In the meantime, the pain in my knee was getting worse. One day, I went to this new boss. He was an Italian man in charge of over 300 people. He said, "Why do you have pain? Maybe you fell down the step ladder." One time I did fall down, but I was young, I didn't care, I just got up and started working again. I never was worried about the pain.

He said, "Why don't you go to the doctor?" "It costs money," I said. "But we have a company doctor."

So I went to the doctor. He looked at my knee, but he didn't send me for X-ray. This new boss then told me that the doctor said, "It's not that bad. You didn't fall down." He was thinking I wanted to make a worker compensation claim. I wasn't interested about those things. I was young, but I did have pain.

The president of the company always said, "Ottavio, don't worry. You live in your work, you like work. You're gonna be successful." I'll never forget, he put his hand on my shoulder, "You gonna be O.K. because you love to work, you love America." He gave me some speech. I understood him, what he was telling me.

So that's the background. There was a respect over here. I started to like this America. The best part I liked was the excitement. I got to know professional people...doctors...lawyers...they were all nice. In other words, in Italy, the doctor or the lawyer you had to call him, "Sir." Here, when I was doing a job for a doctor, they made me feel so good, equal. I loved this. There was a freedom. It was beautiful. That was the best thing. I stayed in this country for this reason, too.

CHAPTER SEVEN

Meeting Anna

In the meantime, when I had come back to New Rochelle I met Anna. That's the best part of my life. I was at my brother Paolo's house for a party, and I saw this girl. All of the girls I knew were...but she was different. She was so sincere, so nice. I could see that right away. I said, "One day, I gonna come to see you in Connecticut." She was from Waterbury, Connecticut. She had come to visit my brother's wife because they are cousins.

Meanwhile, I was still working in New York City and in Brooklyn on weekends. For two or three months, I didn't see her again because I had to finish the job for Simon. Simon and I became good friends, we talked a lot. He told me about his life. How hard it was for him when he came to this country. How he was a Rabbi, and how he had spent time in a concentration camp. God sent this man to me because he gave me the key to stay in this country. One day, he said "I want to introduce you to my lawyer friend."

I said, "Don't tell me about lawyers." My boss had introduced me to this lawyer. He was doing my immigration

Ottavio DeVivo

papers. I lost so much time and money and he had never given me anything. He was an Italian lawyer, who specialized in immigration. I was working so hard to pay him, but the papers were never done. Even my boss was a little mad, asking, "What's going on with this?" It was hard, years ago, to immigrate over here. When I explained this to Simon, he said I will introduce you to my lawyer, Fred Marcus. Meantime, the lawyer said the paperwork was already filed, and that I had to just wait. But, I wish I'd met Fred before. Fred had a law firm with 3 lawyers on Madison Avenue. Meeting Fred was very, very exciting for me. We got along so well together. Fred is still now my good friend.

Now going back to Carl. He started to retire. I was going to fight. I said, "No," I'll talk to the boss. You leave, I will leave myself." But Carl was happy. It turned out they gave him a good bonus. He said, "Ottavio, I'm O.K. Don't worry, I was waiting. They gave me a good bonus." So he left. I'll never forget him. I have to say he was my guide.

ళం

Now Anna and I started to go out. I used to go to Connecticut on weekends, but I didn't have a car. I took the train. Carl had introduced me once to a man who had a car showroom in New York. I went to talk to this man. He said, "What do you do?" I told him I was a carpenter, a cabinetmaker. He then said, "You want to buy a car? Why don't we do this"... then we worked it out. I did the work, building space dividers in his showroom, in exchange for the car. I then "bought" this beautiful car. It was an Oldsmobile Cutlass Supreme, brand new, dark green. Beautiful! I drove it to Connecticut. I went to see Anna, I wanted to surprise her.

I got on the highway. I wanted to go north, but I went south. I went to Long Island. In other words, I left New York at four o'clock. I reached Connecticut...I think it was ten o'clock at night. When the weekend was over, and I left Connecticut I gave Anna the car because how could I use this car to go to work? It was a sport car. Anna had a car, so I took her car.

I would drive the car to Brooklyn on the weekends and worked there. Simon introduced me to many people. I did a lot of work in Canarsie Brooklyn, but I really didn't like this kind of work (I used to redo kitchen cabinets and finish basements), but I made good money. I was working at the Longines during the week. I was in all these places, and I wasn't getting a lot of rest. If you'd seen me, I was so skinny. I really didn't eat a lot. I didn't have anybody to fix me a nice dinner.

The only time I had home cooking was when I went to see Anna. Her mother was such a lovely person, and she was a really good cook.

Then I rented this nice apartment in New Rochelle. I rented the apartment from this guy who was a little crazy. He would raise the rent often. One Sunday I was in the garage and I was making a little cabinet and gluing some veneer on a table. He saw me working and said, "Oh, you gotta pay another $50.00"

Anyway, I said to Anna, "Don't worry." Then I started to build furniture in Connecticut in Anna's mother's basement. In the meantime, this guy really made me mad. That's when I started to look for a house. But I wasn't married yet. I had time.

It was an idea, to look for a house. I had nice money in the bank. I had a few stocks. Like I said in the beginning, I had stock with utility companies. I bought maybe ten, fifteen utility stocks. Carl had guided me. He said, "You have money in the bank, then you get stock, then you need real estate."

Meantime, I worked very, very hard and I was happy; but I started to have more pain in my knee. When I met Anna, she never said anything. She was a very good girl. When I used to go see her in Connecticut, she'd see me limp, her brothers would see...but they never said anything. They thought I had this from Italy, when I came, but that's not true. When I was in Italy, I was in the army, things like that. But the only thing... maybe I pushed too much here. Anyway, I went to another doctor in the city. I told Anna and her mother said, "Look, there is a good doctor here in Waterbury, Connecticut." He was an Italian doctor. We made an appointment.

Anna went with me and we sat in front of him. It was funny. I said, "Look, I have a pain in my knee." He took an X-ray and said, "You have a problem with your hip, not your knee. You need an operation." He scared me a lot with that. He said, "We have to cut the bone, and we have to put a pin in it."

I liked this doctor, but the other doctor in New York never told me this. Anyway, I said, "The pain is gonna go away after the operation?" He said he was confident that the surgery would go well, but he said there were no guarantees in life. He couldn't even guarantee he'd be there. He said he had a very bad heart condition. Anyway, Anna was so scared. We were going out, but I hadn't given her a ring yet.

In the meantime, I was feeling at home in her house. I used to go to see her on the weekends.

One day, I was talking to Simon and I told him I had to have an operation. He said "Ottavio, if it has to be done, do it right away."

My brains were a little confused. I worked hard in the night, doing this and this; and then I was thinking about having the operation. I called Italy because the doctor asked me if I had any problems with the leg when I was small. I told him I had a problem, during the war in 1942, when I was in this tunnel. I was about five years old. I had pain in the leg, but then it disappeared. I was sick for a couple months, maybe a year, I don't remember. Then I said, "Let me call my mother and ask her what leg it was when I was sick." She was so cute. She said to me, "It's the leg that hurts you now!" Anna was laughing. "Your mother is a big help!" she said. Still now we make a joke of it.

Anyway, I made the decision to have the operation in Waterbury, Connecticut. I had surgery in December of 1967. I told my boss. The decision was made. The doctor said again, "You're not going to have any more pain." I was concerned because little by little I could see the muscle in my leg was getting thinner. There were a lot of things in my brains. But, I made the decision. I asked Anna's mother if I could recuperate with them. You know, I began treating her like a second mother.

I found a very good family. Orlando and Louie, Anna's two brothers were so nice. They accepted me in the family. I felt very good. When I meet Anna, she had lost her father a couple of years before. Now it was just her and her mother in the house. Her brothers were both married.

I trusted this doctor. He looked very serious. The operation was a good success. I was in the hospital for a week. Now I needed to recuperate. I was walking with a crutch. My boss had my friend, the Italian translator from New York, come to see me. I was feeling very good. He gave me paid sick leave. My boss came himself later with his wife.

The doctor, after he operated on me, this was like a movie…the poor man died. Exactly one month after my operation, he died of a massive heart attack during an operation. I remember he had told me there were no guarantees in life. He couldn't even guarantee he would be there because of his heart condition. I felt so bad.

The result of all this is that the surgery was a success and I did not need therapy. After two months, I went back to New York and to work. At first I went to work on crutches. I had three men working for me. My boss trusted me. Meantime, I'm going all around the building and doing the furniture on the side. The pain came back and I realized I couldn't do this anymore, these part-time jobs. My boss had said, "You can work all the overtime you want. I was working until 11:00 o'clock at night, but most of the money went to the government because I didn't have anything to deduct. Nothing I could do.

Meanwhile, I was going back and forth to Connecticut and things were becoming a little bit serious with Anna. Then I gave her the ring and things were more than a little serious. I'll never forget, we went to the beach in Milford, Connecticut. This is where Carl had his summer house. This beach brought me good luck because we sat on the sand and I said to Anna

...I was shaking. I was a little scared. I never was so serious about marriage. I knew that she was the person I wanted in my life. I knew I was on the right track..."Will you marry me next year?" "Why next year?" she said. Well, anyway, we set the date. My family was over in Italy, but my father came for my wedding. My mother couldn't come. He made me so happy. It was so beautiful. He said, "Ottavio, you did the right thing. You got some girl!" My wife fell in love with him and it was nice.

Wedding with Anna Romeo 1969

The wedding was beautiful! I'll never forget it. We fixed the apartment in New Rochelle. I had a good time getting it ready. This made me excited. I put in a new kitchen and things, but he still raised the rent.

We were married on the 4th of July, 1969. And now I have to laugh. I have to tell some things that are funny. The wedding was finished and my brother-in-law, Louie, said, "We gonna go with you. You took my little sister." He said, "I gonna come tonight to the hotel." I hadn't told him we weren't going to a hotel.

We were spending the night in our apartment. We left Connecticut and came to New Rochelle. The landlord was having a barbecue. We parked the car and went up to our apartment. I was feeling so happy.

Then, son of a gun, I heard loud noises outside, I said, "What's that?" I jumped up, looked out the window, and I saw fireworks in the street. I was thinking they did it for us! Then I remembered it was the 4th of July about nine o'clock at night. Anyway, it was funny I really remember this part.

We went on our honeymoon to Miami, Florida. I loved the hotel. I loved the Florida people. We were out for 10 days. The honeymoon was beautiful.

We came back and went to Connecticut to see the family. My mother-in-law had a big party for us, but then she got nervous because Anna didn't feel well. Anyway, weeks later we found out she was pregnant. Anna was working for the telephone company in Connecticut and then transferred to the office in New Rochelle. She was a supervisor, but when she became pregnant we knew she wouldn't be there long.

Meanwhile, Fred became a good friend. He lived in New Rochelle about ten minutes from our house. He came to visit us in our apartment. Sometimes I also would also see him in New York.

Now the only thing in my head was to have my own place to work. Something was missing. Yes, I worked at the Longines, I did part time work, but everything was part time. Working for Longines, do this, and do this. I really was pushing.

∞

On April 2nd, 1970, Anna had a beautiful baby girl, Francine. I lovingly call her Francina. Oh my God! I had a daughter! That was my day! She was an angel, beautiful, I couldn't believe it. It changed all my life. Working so hard, I couldn't spend much time with her, but Anna used to take good care of her. She would put pretty dresses on her... I'll never forget, Fred came to see her once, and she had on a pretty dress and pretty little shoes. He said, "Why does she have shoes on, she can't walk." I thought it was so funny too. When I used to come home from work late, I used to see her asleep. I wanted to wake her up, but Anna always said "No". On the weekend, I mean on Sunday, we played all day.

I spent a lot of time at work, but my thoughts were to have a house, to be out of this apartment. We didn't have a lease, so, I said to Anna, "We gotta look for a house." We called a real estate agent, and Anna used to go look at houses during the day. Then at night she would drive me by to see them. Then, she became pregnant again. Great news, but now we really needed to move; the apartment was too small! Anyway, then what happened, a friend in the Longines told me there was a house for sale across the street from him on Pintard Avenue in New Rochelle. This was my friend Al Farry. We later became good friends with Al, his wife, Bernadette, and their son, Paul.

So one night in May of 1971, I went and knocked on the door of the house on Pintard Avenue. It was a big house. I thought, "How much can it be?" That's another part that's funny.

ᔕ

When I was going out with Anna, I used to tease her mother. Oh, she was a wonderful lady! One day I said, "I have almost reached 35." She said, "No, you're not 35." I was meaning I had $35,000. in the bank. She understood that I was going to be 35 years old. It was so funny. Anyway, when I walked into this house, I loved it right away. The key was the basement, that was most important for me. I looked at the basement because the idea was to have space to do some work.

I walked up to Anna and said, "We're going to buy this house." Anna said, "We gotta go upstairs and see the bedrooms." "Ya, but I want to buy it." That's the way I am. When I have a feeling, when you see something you like, you go forward. Anyway, she was so nervous. The owner asked me "How many kids do you have. This is a big house." I said, "I have one and a half, but don't worry about that. I looked at the basement again. There was so much room! But, most important, when I walked in the house, I liked the woodwork, the moulding, the columns. That's what I fell in love with too. Anna loved it too. We went home to talk, and then I went back and gave the owner a check for a deposit. I knew now that I had to continue to work hard. I knew when you want something and you work hard, you're going to get it. That was my feeling.

On August 21, 1971, our son John was born. He was a beautiful baby. We were so happy! Now I had a son and a daughter. I had a beautiful family! And, we were going to move soon into our new house!

We bought the house and my good friend, our lawyer, Fred, did the closing. It worked out very good. With a lot of excitement and with family help, we moved into our new home in October, 1971. Francina was now 18 months old and John was 6 weeks old. The best part was when I told my landlord, "I'm going to move."

House on Pintard Avenue

༙

I worked hard, met more people. Sometimes people paid me more than what I asked because they were very happy. They were satisfied with the work I was doing. And that's what I wanted, to become successful and have a nice family life. You know, you see the future through the kids. I created a family, tried to imitate my father. It's very important in life. The key...and I gotta say this to this new generation... the most important thing is to have a nice family. Money is important, but you have to concentrate on your wife and your kids, your family. The foundation is important. It's like building a house. You pour a good foundation and you will have a strong house (family).

Now we were in the house and I started working in the basement. When we moved into our house, it was one of the happiest days in my life. Anna and I used to live in three little rooms. Now we had this big 10 room house. We had all this room, a living room, a dining room, a play room... very spacious. We painted Francina's room in yellow and John's in blue. We were so happy. My house was open for all our friends, they used to come and visit. I really loved, still love, my house. Anyway, I was working downstairs in the basement now, things were good. Fred had introduced me to an accountant. He was helpful. I was in the right line. Everything was filling in.

I continued to work in the basement at night and on week-ends. Every morning I would get up and take the train to go to the Longines in NYC, but in the meantime, my concentration was on my part time work that I was doing in the basement. I had a lot of jobs. When I got through with a job, I'd say, "What am I doing working at Longines? I don't have any time." I was thinking... but then, you know I was just thinking... I knew it would all work out. I didn't care that I had some pain in my leg and was limping. I was strong, in other words. I was all right. And my life was so happy.

❧

Ottavio takes his young family to Italy 1974
with Anna's mother and nephew LR

When I came to the United States, it took about eight years to go back to Italy for the first time. My goal, when I came over here, was to be successful, in other words, to have a nice life, to get things done in the right way. So, after eight years, I went to see my family. In July of 1974 we took a family trip to Italy. I wanted my family and friends to meet Anna, Francina and John.

You know, it is very tough not to see relatives for so long, but the situation was I had to make some money. I'll never forget...it was very, very emotional. When I saw my mother, my father, my town...there were so many changes.

It was beautiful to see my friends that I grew up with. They hugged me. We talked and talked, they all said, "Ottavio, we miss you."

Ottavio with his mother and father 1974

In the meantime, I still had a problem with my leg and I was limping more. The relatives looked at me, they didn't say anything, but they felt sorry for me. I could see concern in their faces, but they never asked me. They knew I had an operation, but I still had a limp. To me, I was doing alright.

Our trip was beautiful. It was filled with many happy times with family and friends.

When we returned from our trip, I made the decision to become an American citizen like my family. I left my country, this was my new country. I studied all about the United States, so in the fall of 1974, I went to take the citizenship test. I passed. They then brought us to the courtroom where the judge made us stand and we took a pledge. Anna, Francina and John were with me. They gave the kids little American flags and they began to wave them. They were so proud of me, and I was proud too. The United States is a great country.

☙

When we returned from our trip, I met this man named Bob. I met him through a friend of mine. He had just bought a big house on a golf course in Scarsdale, a very nice area. He asked me to give him an estimate for this piece of furniture. He wanted to build a bar. I will always remember this bar. It was big, very big. He showed me pictures. They went on a trip to California and they saw this bar that they liked. They took some pictures. It was like in the West, a real western bar. A very complicated design...and he wanted it in mahogany. I gave him a price of I think...I don't remember exactly...it was around $5,000.00.

Anyway, I gave the price through this friend of mine who worked for him. The man said, "Ask if he could do it for $4,500." $500 less than I had asked. I said, "No, no. Tell him...." Really I could have done it for the $500. less, but that's the trick, the business trick. You have to be very strong. You have to have a good feeling and then give your estimate. My father taught me to give the best bottom of the line, then don't move from that. Don't change. Anyway, after one week, my friend told me to call the man to talk about the price. I said, "No, no way." He said, "You sure? You could lose this job." I said, "To do a good job for him I have to stay at my price."

Then, what happened, the man called my friend. He said, "Ottavio has to be good. He's a good businessman." He gave me the job. I was so happy when I told my wife, when I got $2,500...half the money down... I knew I would be successful.

Now I started to build it in the basement. I had to figure out how to make it in such a way...this big piece...so I could take it apart to install it in his basement. The basement of his house had a small door. I had a small door in my basement too. My brains went nuts. I created it to come apart. Then, when I put it together, it looked like one piece. It was beautiful, just like the pictures he showed me. He loved it.

He loved the bar so much that when we went to his house to deliver it, he gave me another $200. He gave it to me in a bag in five-dollar bills. I put it in my pocket. Then he said, "Let's celebrate." He was a really nice man. That day I had two men working with me to help deliver the bar. It was so big. I had asked my friend, his name is Vito, (he's my neighbor now) to help me. I used to be a very good, close friend to his father. The other man was my friend, Dave, who had introduced me to the bar owner.

He worked for him, and he was using their company truck to help me deliver the bar.

The owner took out a couple of bottles of wine and we started to drink. He was so happy because I built the bar and I was so happy! We maybe drank too much because when we left, the man who drove the truck backed out and bumped into the owner's beautiful Mercedes. We damaged his car but the man was so nice! He didn't say anything. I didn't have insurance for things like this. But, anyway, it all worked out. I came home really happy. I think I was drunk. I couldn't find the way to walk into my house. Vito had to help me. I still had the money in the pocket. I went straight to bed.

∽

In the spring we were blessed with our third child. Our son, Thomas, was born on April 21, 1975. I had a beautiful family. I can't believe it! I had three children. I felt like the luckiest man in the world. Francina was 5 years old, John was almost 4 years old, and our new little baby. Our house was filling up...

CHAPTER EIGHT

Starting my Own Business

When you work hard, the day passes so fast. Now, I had so much work. There wasn't enough hours in the day. I couldn't call my side jobs, part time work anymore, because I could spend all day trying to finish these jobs. Then I started thinking, thinking hard..

One day I went to talk to my boss. The Longines had moved from 47th Street in NYC to New Rochelle when they merged with Westinghouse, and there were many changes at work. They cut back on a lot of things. He was shocked when I said, "Look, Mr. Kerben, I want to leave. I've decided..." He shook hands with me. He was such a good man. He said, "Look, Ottavio, do what you want...but how many kids do you have?" "I have three kids." He said, "What about insurance?" I said, "What do you mean, insurance?" Oh, my head! I wasn't thinking of this. Anyway, I said, "Look, I'm going to leave. How much notice do you want?" He said, "Help us out for awhile. You have three men over here. They need some instructions." I stayed a few extra weeks.

I had a few jobs, so, in July of 1976 I left the Longines. I told Anna that I wanted to concentrate on my own work, my business. She just said "What are we going to do about health insurance?" She trusted me. She never interfered with my decision. She was so good. She always knew that my goal was to have my own business.

In the meantime, because I worked hard, the money came in. I used to take as many jobs as I could. In other words, my idea, my goal, was working. I worked in the basement for over a year.

Then one day I said to Anna "Look, I can't work in the basement anymore. I need more room." I looked around and found a building that had two stores. I didn't have a lot of money, but I knew what I had to do. Thank God I had a few assets. I'll never forget, Carl, Simon and Fred and all their advice. They were the three, like angels, who looked over me. All my life they helped me.

Anyway, I went to look at this building at 764 Main Street in New Rochelle. When I showed Fred, he wasn't too excited. He didn't like that I would have apartments upstairs. I trusted his opinion, but I really liked this building. It was a brick building, it had four rental apartments upstairs, and two stores downstairs. I was very, very excited. I didn't think twice. As I always did when I make up my mind, that's it. I gave a deposit to the realtor. Anyway, I bought the property in December of 1977. I was so happy to move. I had my first commercial property. It had two stores, both were rented. One tenant had to move out because I needed the space for me.

After the closing, oh my God! Believe me, one night I stayed over there all night. Anna said, "What are you doing over there?" It was more like my house. I spent more time in this building, my new shop. We went looking for new machines. We went to New Jersey, to this dealer who sold special machines. We spent almost the entire day there. I then made my decision as to what machine I wanted and went downstairs to sign some papers. The man said, "Ottavio, how are you gonna pay?" I said, "Look, I'll give you cash." Then I paid and said, "Come outside, I have my three kids with me."

He was thinking I had three kids working for me. He was surprised to see Anna, with the three small kids in the car, waiting. That's why I have so much respect for her, we worked together. We did things together. She was always there for me, she was my brick. We brought the new machine back with us. I put it in the shop, and then started building large cabinets.

გ

There was a nice neighbor by the building on 764 Main Street. I used to talk to him a lot. He helped me when he said "You bought this building? You're the one? You're so lucky! You are on Main St., you know how many people pass in front of your store." He was so right because I would put things in the window, and really so many customers would come in. So, I'll never forget this man. The poor man died with cancer of the bone. I used to go see him

When he became very ill, he was in the hospital and I went to see him. I said "What can I get for you? Is there anything you want?" He said, "Ottavio I want some shrimp." I went to the store and bought shrimp cocktail, and took it to the hospital. He ate it and said, "Ottavio, I don't care if I die tomorrow. I got what I wanted!" I'll never forget. Things like this make me feel good now. After he died, I could still see him eating the shrimp.

છ૭

I continued to work very hard but I missed my family in Italy. So, we decided to take another family trip to Italy. This time there were five of us. So, in the summer of 1979, we went to Italy again.

Second trip to Italy 1979

It was, again, very emotional to see my parents who now were so much older. We visited with all the family and friends. Thomas, who was only four, played with all his cousins. He didn't understand them, but they all ran around and played. I thought playing is international.

I wanted to show Anna and the kids the southern part of Italy. We rented a car and started our trip south. We drove and stopped at different beaches in Calabria. We drove along the coast and then took the ferry into Sicily.

When we were in Sicily, I remembered my father loved white wine. So, I bought a case of homemade wine at a private home near Mount Etna, the volcano.

We went to the beach in Taormina, Silicy. We visited the volcano, Mt Etna. We had a fun trip. We stayed at a beautiful hotel with a large pool. The kids really enjoyed this trip. Later, when we returned to my father's house, my father asked Thomas, "What do you like the best in Italy?" He was hoping Thomas would say his house, but Thomas answered, "Sicily." He loved the hotel pool. Our three week vacation went by too fast. It was very hard to say good-bye.

When we returned to the States, I tried to make the business stronger. I kept the store next to me rented. I didn't want to let this man go. He repaired windows and screens, and he was so nice. He said, "Ottavio, I'm over here for many years…" People thought he owned the building because he was there for so long. We became good friends.

❦

I once had one customer, she was so bad. I'll never forget.

For her, when you built a kitchen, she wanted you to repair her entire house. I gave her a nice estimate. I did the job, but then she expected me to fix the rest of the house. She wanted a new floor made...she wanted almost the whole house repaired, but she didn't want to give me any more money. The estimate I gave her was just for new kitchen cabinets. I didn't want to call Fred. But, anyway, to make the story short, I worked it out. My helper, Pete, and I spent one month to do the best for her. I then bought her a bottle of wine and finished. I lost a couple of thousand dollars on the job, but in the end she paid me.

❦

I then started to make furniture: armoires, wall units, bookshelves, tables, and chairs. The store was getting crowded, so 1981 I rented another store to sell the finished and unfinished furniture. I was at 764 Main Street and the rented store was at 618 Main Street. Anna used to help me out. She used to go to the new store and the kids would go there after school. John, Francina, and Thomas played in the store. It was fun for them. I had a lot of customers. But, I was moving from one place to the other.

I met this man through Fred. He was so good. Stitch was his name. On Saturdays he used to help me deliver furniture. He was not only a delivery man, sometimes he was my sales helper. He was always helping me, giving me guidance. He became a good friend. I loved this man. He was so nice! Anyway, he told me that I needed more space to work. He never pushed me to do anything. He'd say, "You gotta do it yourself." This made me start thinking...

∾

One day, Simon came to my house to visit. He brought me a tree, a small tree. He gave it to me because he said it was in front of his house and his son-in-law said it had to be moved. I planted it near my garage. Not long after, Anna invited him and his wife and his daughters to dinner. Anna made a delicious spaghetti dinner. We had a good day together. When they were leaving, Simon looked at the tree, touched it and smiled. You can't believe it, still now, 35 years later, how much I love it! It's my good luck tree. It looks like a Christmas tree. Every year I pay the gardener to trim it. I love it, I love it!

Fred was always with me. He was always watching out for my legal things. He explained how I needed insurance for when I delivered cabinets, and helped me get it. He was watching all these things. He was always looking out for me. We used to help each other out. He also knew I was always there for him. He was and still is a very special "Amico" (friend). In life, when you have a friend, he can call you, you can call him, you can talk...feel comfortable with what you have to say. It is very special. He helped me a lot.

My business started to get bigger. I hired another man to work for me. He was from Jamaica. I now had Pete and Marshall. They were really good workers.

I'll never forget, we would start work at seven o'clock in the morning and work till five o'clock. My leg started bothering me, but I didn't look at the pain. I was limping, but I never complained.

Rabbi Simon Kornbluth's Lucky Tree

&

In 1983, I was working at 764 Main Street and selling furniture at 618 Main when I came across another building. It was at 52 Drake Avenue. The building had five apartments and one store and a two-family house with a garage in back. I wanted to buy it because of the garage in the back. I needed a location for some new machines I had bought. Machines that where too big for the store where I was, but important to build the type of furniture I was building. I knew they would fit perfectly.

So I bought the building on Drake Avenue. I re-did the apartments and fixed the shop in the back garage with the new machines. I was all the time improving the business. I used to take so many jobs, and now I was making all these kitchen cabinets. I made so many kitchen cabinets, you can't believe it.

❧

The kids were starting to get big. I all the time was thinking that I wanted to send them to good schools. We sent them to private Catholic schools. I was living a normal American life. Anna was born in this country, but I'll never forget, my Italian friends. They said, "You're crazy! Nobody buys a one-family house, you are an immigrant. You need a two-family house that gives you income."

I was a little disturbed by this, but I didn't say that to anybody. The key was Anna and me. We worked hard because I wanted to give my family the best. I wanted my kids to grow up in a nice area. I was in this nice house. That was it. We were doing OK.

We decided to join a beach club, The Davenport Club in New Rochelle. I wanted my kids to go swimming, to have a nice pool, to have fun. We got together, all my neighbors, and joined the same club. It became a large family fun place. The kids were enjoying it. I'll never forget, Francina swimming. She was swimming so good! John was diving in the pool and Thomas following along. I was so happy. I remembered that I didn't learn to swim until Anna taught me on our honeymoon.

Ottavio and Anna's family: Thomas, Francine and John at Francine's communion 1977

❧

I continued working at the two locations, at 764 Main and 52 Drake, but found it was hard to have two shops not near each other. I couldn't control all the work. So, I started looking around again.

Ottavio's Store 711 Main Street New Rochelle 1985 & 2015

I found this building at 711 Main Street. The building was so big. I said to Anna "Look, we also spend time in the store over there at 618 Main Street. I want to concentrate everything in this one building at 711 Main. I can put a shop on the bottom floor, and the showrooms upstairs." I wanted my own showroom because that was always my goal, my dream. But we had some problems. The architect's estimated to renovate it was close to a million dollars. More than the building cost.

Anna was scared that we couldn't get a mortgage. I knew how much work I had, and was so sure we could work it out. We then went to the bank that we had our savings with. It was called Westchester Federal Savings Bank. We applied for a commercial mortgage. The bank manager helped us with all the paper work, but said that we had to put our house up for collateral. Anna didn't like this. She told us "If you don't pay the mortgage, we could take your house." I wasn't that worried. I knew I had the work, that was the key. My father always said, "When you have work, respect it." My business was like a family. When a customer came into my house, into my store, I thanked them. I was pleased, because they put bread on my table. I all the time respected the customer, like family. I made so many connections, they became my friends. So, I bought 711 Main Street in 1985. It was a real risk, a lot of money, but I did it anyway.

Next to this building was an empty lot. My customers would come to the store and they couldn't find a place to park. So the next year, I said to Anna "Look, I want to buy this piece of land because customers need to park." They would say, "You don't have a parking lot?" So, I bought the lot, this is the key, it was to help the business grow. Anyway, everything worked out good. The architect did some beautiful drawings for the new parking lot. It cost a lot of money, but I felt it was important.

CHAPTER NINE

My children Grow...and Then Grandchildren!

John and Thomas had a lot of friends who, like them, liked to play music. They used to come to practice at my house. They took over my basement. John played drums. Thomas played bass. They created a band.

At night, you had to see my ears! Sometimes, we got a little upset. When the friends used to pass through the kitchen to get to the basement, I would look in their faces. It was very important to see who their friends were. I wanted them to feel at home. I didn't want them to go hanging out some place, but they were all good kids. Anna and I always said we bought a big house for our kids to enjoy.

So, the way I feel and the experience I have now, makes me want to write this book, to tell other people what it means when you feel you have to do something. You have to have a lot of guts, and the key is to catch the right woman and then love each other. Anna and I talk. We sit down at the table and talk. Anna is so terrific. Sometimes we make mistakes, but we learn from mistakes.

The kids started to get big and Francina was looking at colleges. She applied to several schools.

She was a terrific girl. She had a very good foundation. She went to the Ursuline School, one of the best private high schools in New Rochelle. I remember the principal of the school talking to me and Anna and saying, "She's so good." That made me feel so proud. I told Anna that I don't care what college she goes to, I don't care what it costs, we'll pay for it. That's what we did. The key is give to the kids what is possible, so they can make a future for themselves.

When she graduated high school, we were so proud of her. I decided I wanted to buy her a car. I bought her a Mustang convertible. I'll never forget, it was her graduation day when we went to pick it up. What a story!

When we picked up the car, there was no gas in it, so it took us longer to come home. The car stopped and we had to walk to a gas station. We lost about a half an hour. As soon as we drove in the driveway, Francina looked at us. She was upset. She was so cute. She said "Dad, I gotta go to my graduation. I have to pick up my friend and now we are going to be late." Anyway, I had the key in my hand, I said, "Francina, look!" I gave her the key. Then she saw the car. Then everything changed. She then drove herself and her friend to the graduation in the new car.

The car was really nice, and she deserved it. We were happy because it was really nice to see her happy. Graduation was beautiful. I will always remember how proud and happy Anna and I were. We always tried to give the kids the best. It is beautiful to see how close Francina is to her brothers. We have a very good family. They reminded me of my family, the way they would talk to each other. It was like a mirror.

Francina had friends all around her, everybody came to the house. Anna and I used to watch and say, "Look how nice it is to see Francina, John, and Thomas and their friends all around." I knew when I bought this house this was the foundation for our family. Working hard is the key, but the hope for the future is to keep the family close. That's the key. We were very lucky.

Francina was a beautiful girl. Still now she's beautiful. Anyway, now things were going to change. She was going off to college. She chose Syracuse University.

So in September of 1988, we brought Francina to Syracuse University. Syracuse University was a beautiful place in a very nice city. We brought Francina to her dormitory, and I was a little disappointed. The dorm had boys and girls. When I saw there was a boy living across the hall from her, I said "What's going on?" Anna talked to me calmly, and said "Don't worry. Your daughter knows what to do." I was a little bit nervous.

Anyway, as we left the dorm, Anna started crying. I said, "Anna, you remember when you lived in Connecticut with your mother? Then we married and you moved to New York. You cried because your mother was far away? That's life. That's the way it goes." Then I convinced her, and we went home. Francina's first year was terrific. She loved it! She met a lot of kids and made some good friends. She makes friends so easily.

We used to go to Syracuse to visit. This is very important. That's the point I want to make. We went to see how our daughter was doing, and to meet her new friends. My friend, Simon would say to me "Ottavio, it's very important, you have to meet their friends."

By Thanksgiving of the first year, Francina met...this made me very happy, me and Anna, because she met this boy by the name of Rafe. I'll never forget, this...man, when he came to my house the first time. He had a nice look, and he was very, very nice. Then he would come to visit Francina and he would stay at my house. I treated him like a son. My daughter was so happy. I could see them together, in other words.

The next year, September of 1989, John went off to college too. He went to Le Moyne College, also in Syracuse, to study business. The key for the kids now was to concentrate on their education. But now, I had another big...I call them "mortgages"...the college mortgage. I wasn't scared. Anna was managing my business and I worked hard. Everything was good.

Now we went to Syracuse to visit both Francina and John. We would take them and their friends out to eat. The key was their friends. To have a good family, good kids, you have to follow them. You have to talk to them. Anna got an 800 number so they could call home. It worked out well. They did well. I was lucky.

When John was in LeMoyne, he met this girl, Shawn. Nice girl, beautiful girl. It's funny because she came from New Rochelle too. Francina, Rafe, John, and Shawn were all living in Syracuse. They sometimes would see each other. They became very close.

Francina was still going out with Rafe. I said, "It's good. No problem." What counted to me was that he respected her. The funny part, it was...I am Italian and I was worried that our culture was so different...but, that's the key in this world, to let your children grow. Let them find who they like. You can't push them, they have to do it by themselves. This makes me think of my father who used to say all the time: "The water on the top of the mountain finds its own way to go down."

Anyway, one time we went to Syracuse and we met Rafe's father and mother. I liked them from the first time we met. I felt very comfortable with them. We then met Rafe's sister, Kate, and his grandfather. Such a nice family. After awhile things got serious, and the families were blending. The Bennetts lived in Maryland, but we used to get together.

Francine graduated from Syracuse University in May of 1992. I was so proud of her. It was such a special weekend. After Francina graduated she looked for a job. She had graduated with a dual degree in Elementary and Special Education. One day she went on an interview in the Bronx. They offered her a job working in a Special Education class, and she accepted. It was in a really bad area, but she was excited. She said "Dad that is my job, to teach these children." That's my daughter, she is so special. We knew she couldn't drive and park her new car there, so I bought her a messed up car. The motor was good, but the body was damaged.

The principal of the school fell in love with her, because she was so dedicated. She was doing a lot of things with the kids. She said "Dad, they're so cute. I have such a nice class." We were so proud of her.

එ

The next year, 1993, Rafe graduated from Syracuse University, I'll never forget. His grandfather came for the ceremony. He wasn't a young man, and there were a lot of steps in the stadium. We worried he could not make it up to the top, but he said "I came here to see my grandson graduate." This man, he had a lot of guts. He went all the way up to the top. I followed him up and then said to Anna "I have a lot of respect for this man and this family." Later that day, I told him I liked his tie. I said "Do you like my tie? Why don't we exchange ties?" So we did! I'll never forget this. I really admired him.

Now both Francina and Rafe were working. Rafe was in the army, and came to visit as often as he could. Then on Thanksgiving Day in 1993, Rafe and Francina got engaged. He asked me for her hand. He was so nervous. He walked in and out of the room, and then asked our permission. We were so happy!

They then started to plan their wedding. They set the date for December 18, 1994. Rafe was now stationed to Fort Carson in Colorado Springs, Colorado. They didn't see each other very often, and I could see Francina really missed him.

એઝ

In the meantime, I started to go to shows and furniture convention in the U.S. and in Italy. I went to shows in Milano and Verona. I started bringing furniture from Italy to sell in the store. The shop and store were now at 711 Main Street. I started to introduce a new line of furniture, new things. It worked out well. The only thing it created more work, more pressure on me and Anna. But it was… what the hell…we did it.

The good thing about all my trips to Italy was I would always stop to see my mother and father. They were so happy when they saw me. It was so sad to see them slowing down. I lost my father first, and a few years later I lost my mother. My trips to Italy were never the same...

Tommaso and Assunta with her homemade pasta, mid 1980

I have so many experiences, so much I learned from my father. All the time I would ask him for advice, what kind of machines or something. He would always say "Ottavio, I have a lot of trust in you. You will make the right decision." I was always putting him on top. "I wish I could be like you Papa." And he would say "No, no you are better than me." Same thing now I have so much trust in Francina, John, and Thomas. It's a feeling. It's something that you get. I know that whatever they do they always make me proud.

Luisa and Giovanni DeVivo with Ottavio in Serino

Ottavio with his mother 1995

My father also taught me respect. Don't take advantage of a situation or advantage of other people. He would say "Don't do anything bad to someone, because you don't want someone to do bad to you." That was his idea. Respect people, be close to them. That's how we brought up the kids.

I miss my friends in Italy. When my mother and father were alive, I used to visit with them too. I had a close friend there who would always say "Ottavio, I wish you were still here." I came to this country and made new friends, but my old friends are very important. I miss them, but if I had to do it again, leave Italy, I would. I left Italy and created a new life over here. It's like I have two lives. Sometimes, inside me, you don't know how much this bothers me. Still now, I think of them. I call them, we keep in contact. One of the most important things in life is a friend. My father used to say, "When you find a good friend, you find money in the bank." The key is, don't lose your friends.

෨

Business was OK, but I never wanted my sons in my business. I always thought...if it happens, it happens...My idea was they should have time and space to do whatever they wanted after college. But, when they were home, they used to work with me on weekends and in the summertime. It was a base we created. I told Anna to forget tomorrow. You never know. "Che sara, sara."

෨

John graduated from LeMoyne College in May of 1993. I can't believe it! It was fantastic! We had a fun weekend celebrating. We now had two children graduated from college. I was so proud. Shawn and John were still going out together, and she also came to the graduation. And, our Thomas was going to start at Syracuse University in September of that same year. Life was so good.

Just before graduating, John said "Dad, I want to work with you." That was a good thing, you see. It made me happy, but it also worried me. I thought what will happen to my son if I don't have work? He said "Dad I want to do it." I said "Try it. I'll give you one year. If you like…"

At the same time as my son came to me, I had a friend down the street who had a big business. I went to see him, and when I went in his wife was crying. I said "What's wrong?" The son was so mad at his father. They were fighting. I said, "Oh my God! I don't need this now." I was so scared. I went home and told Anna. "What are you worried about? That is not your son!" And then…I said "Well maybe it's different, but it scares me." Anyway, it worked out. I let John try it, and in one year, he was doing so good!

෴

Meanwhile Francina was busy planning the wedding. The date was set for December 18 and the place was picked. The reception was going to be at the Stouffer Hotel in Westchester. It was a beautiful place. Francina was happy, Rafe was happy, we were happy. We were getting a third son. The wedding day came, the weather was perfect. The wedding was beautiful. The reception was fantastic. Everyone had a wonderful time!

Then, after the wedding, they left. They went to Colorado.

I was so proud. I didn't know where Colorado was, so Anna and I went over there to visit in January of 1995. It was a long plane ride. They had bought a town house. I couldn't believe it, they just got married! It was a beautiful house. They fixed it up so nice. They lived there for a few years. Francina taught in the elementary school on the army base. She also went to the University of Colorado and got a master's degree in Education. Then they came back from Colorado. She was pregnant and they started looking for a place to live.

Rafe had finished his five years of service and was accepted at the University of Maryland Business School, so they looked for a house in Maryland. They decided to move into Rafe's grandmother's farmhouse in Ellicott City. This was Rafe's father's mother's house. She had died the year before.

This farmhouse, some of which was 200 years old, was very nice, but very old. I'll never forget this house. It needed a lot of work. We used to go to help, like my father used to do too. I'll never forget fixing up the kitchen, painting the cabinets, putting in new countertops. The kids were great, they worked so hard. Poor Francina was pregnant for her first child, and Rafe was working and going to school, too. I knew it would be fine. Anyway, they fixed it up. Francina and Rafe, together, the things they did. They made things so perfect, so beautiful. I couldn't believe it. Everything worked out. They made everyone who came to visit feel welcome in their home.

Rafe's parents helped out in many ways. We worked together. They helped, Ralph and Carol, good people. I never had an argument. I used to treat them, and still I treat them, like my family.

And then I realized, going back to my son-in-law, that he was so good. He was a hard working man. I said, " Rafe, you're gonna make it." When he was in the army he was a Captain. I'll never forget, he took me inside this tank. I said, "Look, the control, the responsibility you have." Later, when he got a job with General Dynamics, these people understood. They knew this man knew so many things. Tanks cost a million dollars, and he was responsible for them. And, so far, he's terrific. I'm so proud. But the key is him and his wife, together.

It was so beautiful to see my daughter so happy. They had the baby's room all ready, and then their first child came. Owen was born September 23, 1997. When the baby came, oh my God! I was so excited! I missed the first train from New York to Maryland, so when I got there the baby was born already. It's hard to describe to somebody what it means to have a grandchild...just beautiful! Rafe, his father and I, were so happy! They created a new generation. And that's the key. That's the story, it's the beginning of their family.

c/o

Now I see Francina taking care of Owen. He's a terrific boy...beautiful. He is so intelligent. She takes good care of him. She is an educator, she will teach her son. It's very important for the mother to take care of her kids. It's the key for a good strong family. Teach them respect.

Life is not too easy. Teaching your children is number one. The key is: the father and mother have to work with their kids, teach them about life. They have to be "like" friends. They can't be just "I'm the father." "I'm the mother." Kids have to do things for themselves. There's no question about it. Like my father did with me, but I always want to be their friend.

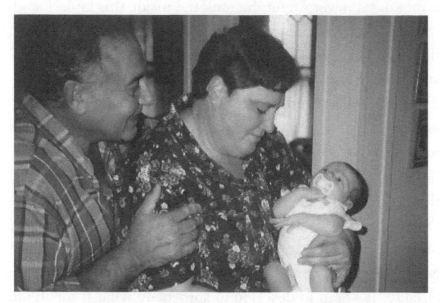

Ottavio and Anna became Nonno and Nonna
with the birth of Owen 1997

We have to let them grow. That's very important. I learned that from my wife because sometimes I'm a little tough guy. Sometimes I don't have patience. I see something wrong, and I tell them right away the way things should go. Sometimes, I don't think when I talk. But the key is, you have to listen to them. They have to make the best of their lives, like we did. But, the one thing that is important, you have to respect them. I love my children. I have three children and nobody in the world can say anything about them.

After working with me for several years, John told us he and Shawn wanted to get married. Shawn was now teaching and doing very well. They set their date for July 3, 1998, a Friday, the day before our 29th anniversary. What a 4th of July weekend we're going to have!

So on July 3, 1998, we had another big, beautiful wedding. It was a beautiful summer day, everyone was so excited and happy. We all danced, we ate, and had fun. Even Owen came for a short time. We now had more family, the Davidsons. The Bennetts on one side, and the Davidsons on the other, Eileen and Gary and their daughter, Brooke. We get along very well. The key is the respect. I respect them, I respect their daughter and they respect my son. That's the key. We want to see the kids happy.

ℰℳ

Going back now to John, I was scared, but it worked out well. He liked, he loved, I could see him love it the way I love woodworking. Plus he's good with his hands. He's good with his brains. He displays things nice. I said, "Oh, that's good." Then I started being happy, more relaxed.

My Thomas loves art, he always did. He studied Industrial Design in Syracuse University. He paints, and also creates different art designs. When he was in school, sometimes he would come home to get some special materials for his projects. Then he started to work with wood. The only thing, I was so upset. They had big new machines at the university, but they didn't ever use them. The school was afraid the kids will cut their finger, like me when I was learning. Thomas told his professor that he had worked in our shop. So, one day, when he came home, he told me that his teacher said, "Thomas, you can use these machines, but watch yourself." I was glad. How can you create things if you don't use all the machines?

Thomas graduated from Syracuse University in 1998 with a degree in Industrial Design. I was so proud of him. His graduation was on Mother's Day. What a beautiful weekend! We all were there, even Owen. What a year...another college graduate in our family (our third) and we were getting ready for a July wedding!

John is now about five years working with me and now Thomas wants to come in the business. He loves to design furniture. I guess he grew up with it and he is very good at furniture design. Oh my God! Another scare, I said. "What are we going to do if we don't have work?" But, it turned out, thank God, I had work. He came to me like John did. I didn't push them to come to me. It's what they wanted. He said, "Dad...." It was beautiful. "I'd have to go work for somebody else to use what I learned in college. I want to put it in the business." And, so far, John and Thomas get along very well. Thomas does the drawings, they talk together...they give an estimate. They work hard. And that makes me happy.

My sons are so special. My family is so special. Our family continued to grow. Francina and Rafe had their second son, Christopher, on April 6, 2000. And then the next year, Shawn and John had their first child, Tessa. She was born on July 25, 2001. We now had three grandchildren. This makes you think about life in a different way. You love the grandchildren. You love your kids. It's amazing! It's a good feeling is what I'm trying to say.

လ

Thinking back to Italy makes me remember how Francina got her name. She was named after my uncle. When Anna was pregnant, we discussed names and I said, "Anna, if it's going to be a boy, I would like to name him Francesco, Frank." But it was a girl, and then we came up with the name Francine. Anna was so good to me, and let me pick out the baby's name. She knew that this man, my father's brother, was very special to me. When Anna was in labor with Francina, she had a dream. And, believe it or not, she said, "I saw three men." She saw her father, who had died, a dear family friend, and a man with a mustache who she did not know. It was amazing. She saw my Zio Francesco. I thanked her so much. He was a good man, and Francina, she's a good girl.

Now John, John was named after my first brother, Giovanni. I have a lot of respect for him. My brother got the name Giovanni because it was our grandfather's name. I never met my grandfather, but I always heard he was a good man. When John graduated from college, he went to Europe. He went to see my family, and met my brother, his Zio Giovanni. He loved it over there. He traveled with a friend and his cousin Angela. I was so glad he met the family.

Then, when Thomas was born, I said, "Anna, what are you going to name him?" She is such a good person. She said, "O.K. I'll make you happy again." And we named him Thomas, after my father Tommaso. He already had two grandsons named after him in Italy, but this is what we wanted to do. My father called him the "Thomas of the United States of America." That's the whole thing, in other words, I believe in tradition.

Nonno Tommaso with his 3 Tommaso grandsons

❧

Every year I used to go in Florida in the wintertime, and I played bocce with friends. One day this man, who had just had a hip operation, walked by. He said, "Why do you have a limp?" Then what he said made me think. He said, "They can fix your leg." I told him I had an operation a really long time ago. And now, this man...this friend, made me think. I went to his doctor in Florida. He took X-rays. He suggested a hip replacement. So, when I came back to New York, I said, "Anna, I'm thinking about having an operation on my hip, but I want to find a doctor in New York."

A few years earlier, this doctor, from New York, had gone to Italy, to my hometown, to find his roots. His last name was DeVivo too. (our last name means "of life") He met some people, distant relatives, who told him that there was a DeVivo, a Ottavio DeVivo, living in New Rochelle. When he came home he called me. We went out to dinner and had a great night. We are distant cousins, and he looks like me a little bit.

He practiced at Columbia Presbyterian Hospital in New York City. We talked and talked, and even talked about my leg. He said he'd give me the name of an orthopedic doctor. I made an appointment with this doctor, and I went to see him. I took the X-rays with me. I didn't like him too much because...I don't know why. I was looking for something inside me, something to make me feel comfortable. When you feel things, it's very important.

Then I went to see another doctor at another big hospital in New York City, The Hospital for Special Surgery. I liked him right away. I looked at his hands, and I saw the hands of a sculptor. I said to myself, this is the doctor who is going to do my operation. I felt very comfortable with him. He took more X-rays, I went for tests, and special meetings about hip replacement. So, in April, 2001, he operated on me. He straightened out my leg. Thank God, I walk a lot better, no limp, and have no more pain.

A few months later, I went to a wedding, and a friend said to me, "Ottavio, you really look good. You dance...you walk good..." He said, "Why didn't you do it years ago?" I said, "Years ago I was concentrating on work, I had a business to run." In life, you make a lot of sacrifices to do what you have to do. When I used to work hard, I'd have pain, but I supported the pain and it worked out good. I'm so happy now.

~

One day, I came up with the dream of my life. I used to go to Florida and stay in my brother-in-law Louie and his wife Brenda's condo. Now Anna and I decided to buy a place in Florida. We found a condo in Jupiter, next to her family. My wife fell in love with the fountain in back of the condo, we had to have it! So, we bought the condo in August, 2002.

Anna and Ottavio in Florida

I was thinking that all the family could enjoy it. I'll never forget, we fixed it up a little bit, and then shopped and shopped. That Christmas, when we got together, we exchanged gifts. We bought beach towels for everyone and gave them each a trip to Florida.

Francina and Rafe came to Florida with the boys. They loved the pool. Owen and Christopher had such a good time. When I saw them playing, I felt so good.

In April of 2003, John came with Shawn and their two kids, Tessa and Luke. Luke was born in October, 2002 and was only six months old on his first trip to Florida. I loved it. I always say, "If they're happy, I'm happy, too."

What I'm saying, this comes from my heart. My kids are good kids. I don't tell them what they have to do. They have to find their own way. Just like: "The water on the top of the mountain finds a way to go down by itself." You cannot stop it. The kids have to do for themselves, because tomorrow they will have to face situations for their children. They need to be strong. I say all the time, "It's a job to raise a family, just like a business. I'm a businessman and a father, I have made a lot of decisions, and I know my kids will make good family and good business decisions.

CHAPTER TEN

My Trips

One day I was talking to Carol, Rafe's mother. She said she had information on a trip to Italy's Lake Region. She said her college, McGill University in Canada, was offering this trip. She sent me the information. Let me tell you a little bit about her. She has some instinct, in other words, it's almost...my wife says she's like you, she thinks like you. Anyway, when she sent me the paper, I looked at it and said, "What a coincidence this is..."

When I lived in Milano, I went to Isola di Pescatore in Lago Maggiore. I was young and had very little money, but had told myself that one day I would go back. When I looked at this paper, I said, "Anna, look at this. This is something strange." I was excited and a little nervous. I picked up the phone and called Carol. I said, "Yes, Carol, I want to go on this trip." She said, "I want to go too." She wanted her husband, Ralph, to come too; but when I talked to him, he said he couldn't come because he had to teach school. Anyway, the conclusion, I said, "I'm treating it like a business decision." The key in life is to make a decision. We are going.

About the same time, I was already planning to go to the furniture convention in Verona with Anna. I called the travel agent from the McGill University. He made arrangements for us to go to Italy, to Verona first, and then to Lago Maggiore. What happened, I'm going to describe now. To me this was really unbelievable.

We flew to Verona. Our hotel was next to Piazza Bra, which was right across from the Coliseum. It was beautiful! We spent a week in Verona. We went to the show, a terrific show. While we were in Verona, three of Anna's relatives from Serino came to see us. We spent so much time together. They stayed in the same hotel. It was amazing. It was terrific. I was so lucky with this show. I made so many connections. Anyway, what happened...I dealt with this company...I agreed with them to showcase their chairs in the United States. They made very nice modern style chairs. This company had never exported before.

After I signed the contract with them, I said, "I need a little favor." (I was thinking how are we going to go from Verona to Lago Maggiore?) I said, "We need a ride from Verona to Lago Maggiore." He said, "Ottavio, no problem. I'm busy but I'll send my sister!"

I was so excited, it was like my dream was going to happen. When I was 18 years old I was in Lago Maggiore, now I'm 65. It's was a long time ago. It was for me very emotional. I said to Anna, "I'm a little scared, I'm nervous." She didn't really understand how I was feeling.

When it was time to leave Verona, his sister, Cinzia, came to pick us up at the hotel. We had a beautiful week here. Anna was so happy to see Verona, to go to the show, the restaurants, and see her relatives. It was a present to her to go to Verona and Lago Maggiore because she's a very hard worker. Most of the time I would go to Italy myself, and Anna would take care of the business. But, this time I wanted to give her something special. The key is you have to share things with your wife. It's a beautiful feeling.

On our way to Lago Maggiore, we stopped in the city of Vicenza. Cinzia said, "You have to see this amazing building." It was the building, The Villa Capra. The four sides of the building all look the same, identical! The house has four front entrances. A very rich man built it as a party palace in the 17th Century. It was amazing.

It then took over two hours to get to Lago Maggiore. We finally arrived...the hotel was on a hill, it was beautiful.

Cinzia then left, and we thanked her. She was so nice to drive us. After she left, we met all the people from Canada that were on our tour. The only one we knew was Carol, but after two or three days, I knew everybody there. I fell in love with this group. It was so beautiful to be in the middle of all these educated people. Most were doctors. I said, "Anna, we're the only ones who don't have a degree." They were interesting people, such nice people.

When I was in Verona, one of the relatives, who came to see us, brought me a case of wine. They have their own vineyard in Serino. They brought me white wine and red wine... the best wine. I said to Anna, "I want them to take it back. What are we going to do with the wine over here? We can't bring it back to the United States." Anna said, "You can't give it back. They will feel bad. Bring it with us." She's a smart girl.

Anyway, this wine was like gold! When we saw our room...I travel a lot...but this room was so large and beautiful. The view was amazing! We were on the 5th floor and we could see all the islands right in front of us. At night the islands were all lit up, it was even more amazing! I don't know how we got it. Believe me, I had nothing to do with it. I don't know what happened. We were very lucky. Now, I had this wine in my room. Carol and I were talking and she said, "Ottavio, you know what we should do? We should have a party and a glass of wine in your room."

See Carol makes things happen. She organized all these friends, and they came to our room one night and we had a small party.

We went on many tours. Every day they brought us from one place to another. As I said before, we met many different people. There was one lady who had funny hair. She had purple hair. I said, "Son of a gun, I got to talk to her." I introduced myself, and we started to talk. Her name was Louisa, she was so nice. One night she went for a walk with Carol and me into the town of Baveno, just below the hotel. Carol and Louisa talked for half an hour. I don't know, my mind was in a different direction. I was thinking of the past.

We were having a lot of fun. I felt so comfortable with these people. One beautiful day, we went to Isola Pescatore. This is where I wanted to visit. There were things that looked familiar, but there were things that looked so different than I remember. I remembered being here with the people from Milano when I was 18 years old. I didn't have a lot of money I was working and trying to save. It was a different life. I remember getting something to eat from a delicatessen, and sitting on a bench talking to an old man. I remembered the place. It was amazing! To me it was like watching a movie.

I called home the first day we arrived, and my son Thomas said, "Dad, someone called here looking for you. They want to know if you're the people from New Rochelle going on the tour." It was this doctor who lived near New Rochelle, and who wanted to meet us. Thomas told him we were in Italy already, we were in Verona. Now that we were in Lago Maggiore, we met this man. It was Dr. John and his wife, who were looking for us. It was a coincidence. See, all of this, Carol created this, because I met the people from home over here in Lago Maggiore. This John...this doctor... went to McGill University, the same college Carol went to.

Anyway, the day we went to Isola Pescatore, we walked and I talked with the local people. I spoke my language, Italian, and I sang in Italian. Then we went to lunch in a nice restaurant with our tour grop. It was a very nice out-door restaurant on the water. I was looking to eat fish. (Isola Pescatore means Island of Fish.) When the food came, they served us turkey. I thought, Thanksgiving over here in Italy in September. "Son of a gun!" I was so upset. I waited so long to come back here so I could eat fresh fish, but in a group like this, you can't order yourself. Anna said, "Don't worry, we'll come back for lunch another day."

And that's what we did! Our lunch was delicious! We all ordered fish. This was the best feeling, you go someplace when you are young, then go back when things are differ-ent in your life. It was amazing! I was so happy. I enjoyed meeting these people. We toured together, but we also had free time, and everbody did their own thing. I'll never forget.

Carol and John's wife went to the pool every morning. It was late September and a little cool, but Carol had guts. They went in the pool almost every day.

Anna and I now knew almost everybody. We had made new friends. Every day you changed seats in the dining room, and after dinner we would sit in the lounge and have a drink together. One day this man chipped his tooth. I translated for him because he had to go to a dentist. He was very happy.

Good things happen. I went one day with Anna to Stresa. September is the time they have Porcini mushrooms in Italy. I love Porcini mushrooms, and Stresa is the town where they grow. Another coincidence. You see, I believe things happen for a reason. It was Sunday morning and Anna and I were looking for a church because we wanted to go to Mass.

We walked into the church, we sat and who was sitting next to me? John's wife! It was a coincidence. Then I teased her "Where is your husband?" Things like this. "You came by yourself?" Outside, we met John and he and I went to look for a nice restaurant. We found a little restaurant that had a basket of the Porcini mushrooms on display. We went in and I talked with the owner of the restaurant. I bought the whole basket, and he said he would cook special dishes with the Porcini mushrooms. We went back a short time later and ate a fantastic meal. I thought we couldn't eat all of them. But, we did... John, Anna, Louisa and I. That night when we were with the group, we teased everyone and said "You don't know what you missed."

After eating, we walk to the Funicular, Anna, John, Louisa, and I. We went all the way to top of the mountain. It was so beautiful! What a beautiful view! We had a good time that day. We became very good friends with John and Louisa. And that was nice.

Later that night, we decided to have a party in our room again. John had bought wine, and different cheeses. The view from our room was so beautiful at night with the islands all lit up we wanted everyone to enjoy it too.

Near the end of the trip, we went to the island of Orta. I'll never forget Isola Orta. There was this lady on the trip named Rosamund. She had been married to a Belgian diplomat. I saw her crying in the boat as we went to Orta. I said "Rosa! Rosa are you ok?" She said, "I just remember coming over here with my husband all the time."

Orta is a very small island. In the center is the town hall. On the top floor is the office of the mayor. I went up to talk to him. We walked out onto the terrace, and all my friends saw me up there. I waved to them. Me and the mayor on the terrace, everyone laughed. It was so nice. We then walked all around the small island. We bought things. It was an unbelievable vacation!

I also did some business while I was there. I love Pinocchio and there was, in a nearby town, a factory that made Pinocchio sculptures in wood. I had seen all the Pinocchio statues while we walked around in Stressa. I called the owner of the factory, and he came one night to the hotel. He brought me a life sized Pinocchio. Anna was mad. She said "Why do you do this? We are on vacation." I was always thinking about business and bringing some to the United States to sell in the store. I did place an order, and I gave some smaller ones to my grandchildren when I got home.

This trip was something exciting in my life. It couldn't have happened like this, if Carol hadn't gone to college in Canada, if Rafe hadn't met Francina. This was unbelievable is what I'm trying to say.

Another day, we went to Lago di Como. We saw a beautiful church and a museum. Rafe's father had told me there was an important building to see in Como. It was a Mussolini era building, very plain. We went to see it. Nice. I remembered I was in Como when I worked in Brienza. I used to go to Como to enjoy the lake. This day gave me a lot of memories. It was very nice, very exciting.

∾

When Anna lived in Connecticut she introduced me to her good friend and neighbor, John Vassallo. After my hip operation, he called. I was still recuperating. He said, "Ottavio, you want to come with me to Budapest, Hungary and Istanbul, Turkey?" His wife, Tina, was sick, and she couldn't go with him on this trip. I took her place. This is the key. In the life, you have a chance, you have an opportunity, you take it. I said, "Yes," and I went with him to visit his friends in July of 2001.

First we went to Budapest. Then, from Budapest, we went to Istanbul. In Istanbul, he took me to this warehouse. The owner was a friend of John's. I couldn't believe the carpets! My wife wanted to kill me because I bought five carpets, and brought them back to the United States. I was spending so much money in Istanbul that they called Anna from the credit card company. They said they thought somebody stole my card. I just loved this store!

John Vassallo and Ottavio in Istanbul, Turkey 2001

Then we went to a jewelry shop and I bought and ordered jewelry pieces. I was having such a good time. I said, "Look, this is the life. To travel is an education." It was amazing to see this new country. I loved Turkey!

But back to Budapest. We went to eat at this restaurant. I've never had so much brains...lamb brains. I loved them. They were prepared so good, they were delicious. Another day, we went to see this Art Nouveau building. I was interested in this style because I had a customer who wanted me to build them Art Nouveau style furniture, reproduce a table and an armoire. It's amazing what I saw. We also went to the Herend Company showroom. Herend makes very fine hand-painted porcelain pieces. The best in the world. I bought some special pieces for Anna. When I came home, I knew that I spent too much money, but I said, "When am I going to go there again?"

I learned a lot on this trip with John. We had a good time. I was so happy that I went.

CHAPTER ELEVEN

My Life Goes On...

The idea to write this story came when I had the second operation on my hip. The doctor did a terrific job on me, made me walk straight after about 30 years. I woke from the operation feeling O.K. I didn't have any pain! I couldn't believe it! In my room, there was another bed that was empty at first, but in the middle of the night, they put somebody next to me.

The next day, I started talking to him. His wife came to visit that afternoon. She was so caring. Like I said before, the right woman, is the key. We became friends in just a few days. She said, "What do you do? What do you do for a living?" Well, I told her my story. And he was interested, asking questions, you know, the way I do. We talked and talked, we made the time pass, while we lay in this hospital room.

He told me he was a book publisher in New York City, and he gave me his business card. I'm a good judge of people, and I could tell he was a really nice man. Then I got the idea. I started thinking about writing my story, about all the things that happened to me. One day I talked to Carol, and she said she would help me out. She gave me a tape recorder, and the most important thing is...I like to talk. So, I talked and talked and talked for hours...That's how it all started.

Sometimes kids come in the store with their mom and dad, and I like to talk to them. I tell them a story, and I show them the different kinds of wood. I show them the machines, and then tell them to stand back and watch. I take a little piece of wood, and make a little chair for them on the band-saw. The smile on their face is so nice. I'll never forget, one boy sent me a letter thanking me for showing him the shop and for the chair I made.

A few people have asked me, "Why don't you open a school to teach people woodworking?" But, I never wanted to. When I show the kids things, I feel good. What my father taught me, I taught my children, and they will teach their children. It's like a wheel, like a chain.

I talk like this because I have four grandchildren now. The mother and the father have to do the job. Nothing is more important than teaching everything to your kids. Our grand-children give Anna and I (their Nonna and Nonno) so much happiness.

ço

Years ago I first started going to Florida on a yearly vaca-tion, I found it hard to just sit on the beach. I started to be bored. You see, like a said before, I like, I need to talk. One day Anna and I went to the beach. I put some oranges I had bought in the cooler. We sat on the beach and looked at the ocean. Anna was reading a book. It was a beautiful day, and the water was gorgeous.

I saw a man and his wife sitting by themselves. I said to Anna "They look like they are Italian." I went over to them, and gave them an orange. I said, "Where do you come from?" They told me they had come, many years ago, from Italy. We had a nice a conversation. I felt good. The next day, we went to the beach again. I saw another man who was talking Italian to his wife. I go over with another "orange" and start to talk to them. Anyway, to make a story short, by the end of the vacation week, I had the two couples together, talking to each other.

When I came the following year, the group had grown. They thanked me for introducing them to each other. We got together for a picnic. I met so many people! I had a fun week with all of them. The following year, we had a big party, over 50 people. It was so beautiful.

Then a group of us got together and went to the City Hall in Jupiter. We asked if they could build a bocce court near the beach. The approvals took a couple of years, but they did build two bocce courts. So now, we picnic and then play bocce. It's so nice to see things like this. Last year, I bought a whole Prosciutto from my brother-in-law Louie's store, and brought it to the picnic. All the people thanked me, they appreciated it so much. To me, when I see people together, it's something very important. I feel good in my heart. Now that I stay in Florida for the winter, I have so many friends. We have a weekly picnic, and then play bocce.

છ

The weather is bad today, and I just came back from our store. Then I said, "Let me go record in this little room over here." This was John's room when he was little. Outside the window I see the beautiful cedar tree in the front of me. It makes me feel so good to look at it...and then proud in one way. In this house I remember all of the things that I record here.

Ottavio and his wine operation

I'm sitting here with a glass of wine in my hand. Wine that I made myself. My father used to make wine. We would pick the grapes from our little farm, and then we would grind them and make wine. Then when I came to this country, and met Anna, I saw how her brother Orlando made wine here. His father had taught him. So when I bought my house, he taught me, and I started to make my own wine. Each year I became more professional. But the beautiful thing is now John likes to do it too. I stock over 100 bottles of wine in my wine cellar. It is becoming very expensive to make wine because the grapes that come from California are very expensive. But, I love to do it, and I enjoy drinking my wine.

∽

About ten years ago, I was approached by a friend of mine who was a member of the Sons of Italy. He asked me if I wanted to belong to this club. They had a lodge in New Rochelle, so I went to a meeting. I was very happy because I met so many people. Most of the members were woman and I made them feel good. I remember after our meeting I would tell stories, and then I would sing some Italian songs. I enjoyed being a member. After a few years, they asked me to be president. Our lodge worked hard to raise money to give to different charities. And after three years ...what they did, they honored me. It was a wonderful day. I wish my relatives from Italy where here. They gave me a plaque, such a nice presentation. All these people were here for me. It made me so happy. Anna and my kids were so proud. You know, I'll never forget...Francina, John, and Thomas when they came and hugged me and said, "Dad, we're proud of you." These things I will always remember.

∽

We went to Maryland to visit Rafe and Francina. They bought a new house, and had just moved from the farmhouse. I'm so happy for them. They have a lot of nice neighbors around. It reminds me of when I bought this house. The key was the school for the kids, and the neighbors. It turned out good for us because we are in this house over 40 years.

Francina cooked a delicious dinner for Carol, Ralph, Anna, and me. Rafe then opened a bottle of champagne and announced that Francina was expecting another baby. It's so beautiful to see the family grow. Two people, a husband and wife, creating a family. Francina and Rafe are doing a terrific job with Owen and Christopher. Then, on January 8, 2004 little Eric was born. Francina and Rafe now have three beautiful sons, a beautiful family.

કે

Now we have a situation. The people that we met on our Lago Maggiore trip, now they want to have a reunion in Canada. I'm excited. I already made reservations, we're set to go.

So, yesterday morning, I called Dr. John. I said, "John, I'm going to go to Canada for the reunion. Anna and I already made our reservation. Are you and Nadia coming?" He gave me such a speech. "Why are you going now on this Canada trip?" There was a SARS outbreak in Toronto at this time. I said, "John, I know, but we have to die one day anyway." But now I am in this situation. I want to go because they want to have a party over there, a reunion of our trip. It could be beautiful, could be terrific. We'll work it out.

I kept on thinking, SARS is in Toronto. We're going to

Ottawa, which is further away. Life is taking chances, who knows?

What could be more fun than to go to this restaurant in Canada, with these people we met in Italy and have a good time? It feels like I have another family. I am very proud of this. These are friends. Friends are very important. Anyway, we'll see what happens.

ॐ

I had a wonderful day. John and Thomas created this project and I'm so proud of them. It's so beautiful to see the shop and the showroom. Today, I met these people who came in and complimented my sons on the job they are doing. I went upstairs and called Anna. It made me feel so good. It's like the farmer says, "You put in good seed and then, one day, you're going to get good fruit." It takes a long time but that's the key. The key's to spend a lot of time, a lot of concentration. And, with John and Thomas, the business goes very well. They concentrate to make a piece of furniture so perfect. I'm proud. I try to help the most I can. I try to be involved, but really sometimes I get tired, but I'm happy. Happy with what they do.

John and Thomas bought this big machine. They say it's the only one they can work on to create the new style furniture. Anna and I were scared because, sometimes, working a machine, things can happen. But they love to work on it because they get things done perfectly, with precision. The way John has started to do finishing reminds me of my father. When I used to work for him, he taught me finishing. I became very good at it. Then he would say, "Ottavio is the only one to do the finish." I remember his words. It's so beautiful to see what the father created, and the kids take over. It's something very hard to describe.

I tell everybody I don't care if teaching is your profession, if you are a carpenter, a plumber…whatever…just concentrate on your work. When you do a good job, everything is going to feel good in your life.

Now, the big thing is this Canada situation, but I have a lot of trust in Carol. If it weren't for her, I would have never gone back to Lago Maggiore, I would never had met all these people. I look forward to next weekend.

⌘

Fred Marcus, friend and lawyer,
with his wife Nancy and Ottavio

I have a friend I talked about previously, Fred Marcus. Fred called me 10 minutes ago and said, "I want to come over and have some cheese and bread with you." This is amazing because I'm here taping, and I was thinking about him. Then the phone rang and I think, "How nice. That's what it's about...friendship." Fred is a strong man, but he's not feeling well. It's a coincidence that he called, he didn't know Anna was at Francina's and I was alone.

So, we spent time together. Everybody is lucky if you have a good friend. I am very lucky. We help each other in a lot of different ways. I went downstairs, I prepared cheese and bread and fruit. We talked. We talked about family, the grand-children...it's so beautiful...we talked about the past. We have known each other over 40 years. I have learned a lot from him.

❧

Now I look forward to...I can't wait. Next week we're going to leave New Rochelle and go to Ottawa Canada. I look forward to seeing the wonderful people we met in Lago Maggiore. We leave Thursday and Anna wants to spend overnight in Syracuse on our way up.

Finally, it's Thursday morning and Anna and I left New Rochelle and drove to Syracuse. We went to visit everything we remembered from the times Francina, John and Thomas were in college. We went to see the LeMoyne and the Syracuse campus. We stayed in the hotel where we used to stay all the time. They had renovated it. It was amazing, what a change!

Then we went to dinner at the restaurant where we used

to take the kids and their friends. Anna and I sat at the table, we got our drinks, and I said to Anna, "Look at this..." It reminded us of all the times we had here with the kids. And now, two of our kids are married with their own kids, it's just beautiful!

The next morning, we got a phone call from Carol and Ralph. They said, "We're a little distance away, but we'll meet you for breakfast. This is beautiful to get along so well. And that's another key in the life. If the in-laws get along very well, the kids will get along better, and the next generation will learn from this. After breakfast, we left Syracuse and left for Ottawa.

When we reached Ottawa, we went to the hotel, The Chateau Laurier. It was beautiful. I didn't expect something like this. It was like a castle, I didn't expect to stay at a castle! We parked our cars and went to the lobby to check in. Then we went to the dining room for lunch. That afternoon we enjoyed walking around Ottawa.

The next morning we called Carol, and we met downstairs. She introduced us to her relatives who lived nearby and came to see her. We had breakfast together at the Chateau. They were such very nice people.

That night we had arrangements to go to Al and Evelyn's house before we went out for our reunion dinner. It was so nice of them to invite everyone to their home. We went there and met our friends from our trip. We hugged each other, and we talked about the good time we had at Lago Maggiore. We looked at pictures of our trip, we laughed, and then we went out to dinner.

It was Italian Night in Ottawa, and the restaurant we went

to for dinner, Giovanni's, was in the center of the celebrations. We had such a good time. The waiter told Ralph he couldn't believe how much wine we drank. We were a large group, and we were having a good time. It was beautiful. It's hard to describe the night we had. It was really amazing! We even sang and danced. Like I said in the beginning, you can't just lay back and say, "I wish to do this...I wish to do this." That's not the way to do it. It worked out well. Everybody had a good time. I felt bad that John and Nadia were not with us.

On Sunday night, we were invited for dinner at Rosamond. She was our friend who I mentioned before that was married to a United Nations diplomat. Everything in the house was perfect, the antique furniture, the paintings, the dishes, everything. Rosa handled it so professionally. Dinner was delicious. It worked out so well. We had a wonderful night, really.

I'll never forget, I wanted to eat fresh trout. On one of my trips to Italy, I'd heard from the chef at the best hotel in Milano that you should eat fresh trout in Canada. So, I spoke to the chef at the Chateau, and he said he would cook trout for us. The next day for lunch we had trout. It had such flavor. It was out of this world. I've eaten at a lot of restaurants, but this was done so well.

The next day, we had a tour of the city of Ottawa, we even went on a boat ride on The Ottawa River. Everything we did was so good. There was an Italian exhibit in the Museum of Civilization that we saw. It was another experience. It was a beautiful trip. I'll never forget our trip to Ottawa. It was a success! We did all this in three days. It was enough for ten days, but when you want to do something, you do it.

ᘓ

Our family was still growing, our sixth grandchild, Jack, was born on October 20, 2005. This was Shawn and John's third child. I can't believe it! We now have six grandchildren, five grandsons and one granddaughter. God has really blessed us!

ᘓ

It's about 5:00 o'clock on a November day. I'm sitting at the desk taping, and I look out the window...there is a very bad storm.

But, I am very happy because Francina, Owen, Christopher, and Eric are visiting. I am so happy for Francina and Rafe because they have three beautiful kids. Each one is different from the other. I love all three. They are terrific.

I love Rafe, my son-in-law, and Shawn, my daughter-in-law...because I see how nice they are raising their kids and the way they love their kids. Rafe is a very good father. And Shawn...I can see she's a good mother. She takes Tessa, Luke and Jack to visit often.

You see, like I say, it's like destiny, this book, because, if Francina had not married Rafe, I would not have met Carol. Carol is a journalist, and encouraged me to write this book.

It's a week before Thanksgiving, and I am so happy. It's a wonderful holiday. Its family time and we're going back to the table. The table is the key. We're going to spend this... Thanksgiving...all my family, all the six grandchildren, all the family in my house around the table I built.

ҩ

I was thinking today about my mother-in-law. One Thanksgiving, when she worked in a convalescent home, and I was visiting from New York, she said, "Could you give me a ride to the convalescent home?" I said, "Yes." We went there and we picked up this old man...he didn't have any family...and I helped him into the car. In my mind I said, "This woman is crazy!" But, I did what I was told to do. We got in the car and we drove home. She wanted this man to have Thanksgiving around the table with us. It is a beautiful memory.

The second part of what I was thinking...it took years to create my business and now I have John and Thomas...they do a terrific job to continue my business, they are the future for Ottavio's Furniture. Soon I can retire...

It makes me so proud now, when I go in the morning, and I see John and Thomas creating a new style of furniture. It makes me so happy because they create such beautiful furniture. For example, I did work 20 years ago for a customer, furniture for their kids. These "kids" now they come to John, and say, "Your father built this beautiful cabinet when I was little. Now, I would like to give it to my daughter...I would like for you to match the design for another piece of furniture." That makes me feel so good.

Last week Thomas and John designed a big beautiful wall unit for the new technology, the plasma TV. They created this wall unit. I used to talk with people and build cabinets from a little drawing. Now Thomas makes a full-scale drawing and then presents it to the customer. The business has changed. I see all these new machines, all the new technology. They have their future. It is time to give a chance to the new generation.

I get so much enjoyment in going over to the shop and seeing my kids - what they can do. They took over. And then, I think of all the sacrifice, all the investment, I feel proud. They can build things in the United States like nobody else in the world. They can build it because the United States has all the right material, like wood, my trade.

Nobody in the world builds wooden cabinets the way they do in this country. Pennsylvania has beautiful cherry wood. I found out that Italy uses cherry wood from Pennsylvania. I never knew that. Ash wood comes from Massachusetts. Oak, we even have oak in Westchester County.

൭

My son, Thomas, met this wonderful girl. They have been going out for over two years. Good things happen in my family. Thomas became engaged to his future wife, Michelle in April 2007. I'm very proud because he chose this beautiful girl. I don't like to make a judgment, but I'm very good at measuring character. I could see the way she looked at my grandchildren, the way she talked to Owen, Christopher, Eric, and Tessa, Luke, and Jack, not because she's a school teacher, but because she cares about kids. I got this feeling that Michelle's gonna be wonderful for Thomas. I see my son so happy.

The first time we meet Michelle's parents, we went to this restaurant. I remember the restaurant, Graziella's. Michelle's father's name is Hans and her mother is Debbie. Right away, we had a nice connection, we got along very well. A short while later they invited me, Anna, all the family to their house.

They live in the country, a nice area. They have a beautiful swimming pool. I have a beautiful picture that I love. It's a picture of my six grandchildren sitting at edge of the pool. Everybody looks so happy and all smiling.

Water babies Owen, Tessa, Christopher, Luke, Eric, and Jack.

Hans took me in his wine cellar. I always think I have the best wine cellar, but then I find out he has a better one than mine. It was beautiful. He told me a story that there was a big stone. He took the stone out and created this wine cellar. He enjoys it because, after work, he relaxes in there. He doesn't make wine, but buys different kinds of wine from over the world.

Hans...the way he cooked... he looked like an artist cooking. Thomas and Michelle tell me he loves to cook. And I like to eat. You can imagine what a good combination. They are really good people. And I had so much fun with Michelle's grandmothers and grandfather. To me it's like a treasure when you meet someone older than you. They have more experience in life than you. They know more. I was very excited to meet them.

On February 16, 2008, Michelle and Thomas married. A winter wedding, but it was a sunny, mild day in New York. It was a beautiful wedding! So many people, so much fun!

℘

I am so happy with my six grandchildren. I can't be more happy. This makes me feel so good. I said, "Anna, in the beginning, you remember when I was scared when John started working with me and, then, Thomas came? I worried if we didn't have enough work, you know what I mean? But, thank God, when they came into the business, the business grew better because they have younger ideas. That's what I say all the time...the young generation...let the younger generation move on ahead, give them a chance. "If you make a mistake, remember, everybody's allowed to make a mistake."

My father told me, "If you make a mistake, that's how you learn." And that's the key. The key's to see what you can do. But you gotta push, never give up, never give up. Talk to yourself and say, "I gonna make it work."

I come back all the time to my father. I try to give a message for the new generation. My father used to say, "Let it slide. Do day by day. Enjoy your life because...life is so beautiful...let it go like the water on the top of the mountain, let it find its own way." My father is on my mind all the time.

John, Francine, and Thomas 2008 at Thomas' wedding

∽

Question: What am I gonna do when I retire? I gotta retire. I did in my life what I wanted to do, but I still have a lot of ideas. But we bought this place in Florida, and the way I see it, it is not my life. I like to go and spend the winter, but I can't retire in Florida. I think my life is gonna be also in New Rochelle.

∽

It's Thanksgiving Day, 2008. A lot of things happened. Wonderful things. Anna and I have all the family together to celebrate Thanksgiving Day. I gotta tell you the story of what happened this year. Good things happened. After we have a cocktail, Anna says dinner is ready. There's a big turkey in the middle of the table.

Thomas stands up and says, "I have an announcement to make. Michelle is expecting a baby." Wow! It was really, really good news. Everyone congratulated them. They asked me to say a prayer, to bless the food. I stand up. I thank God like I usually do. We pray to God for good health because health is the best thing in the world, and thank God for the good news.

Rafe and Thomas carved the turkey. Anna and I sat at the end of the table and talked about how beautiful it is to see everybody together. That's a real Thanksgiving. The baby...! I called Michelle's father and mother to congratulate them. They're happy too. This is the secret to success, a good marriage. Love is beautiful. It's the key to a strong family. If a family's full of love, you're gonna have a good life, a happy life. It's like a long, long street. Family is everything. Family is the best thing in the world, and this is what it's gonna be for Thomas and Michelle.

So, on June 10, 2009, Michelle and Thomas's baby girl was born. We went to the second floor of the hospital, where Michelle and Thomas were, and then, through the window, we saw the baby. She was beautiful. Thomas said to me and Anna, "You want to know what the baby's name is? Her name is Tavia." They shortened my name. What a surprise! What an honor! What a beautiful name! My heart was very, very happy. I was so touched...and I thanked God for another grandchild. Grandchild number seven.

❧

I am in Florida in December 2009, with Anna, Francina,

Rafe, Owen, Christopher and Eric. We are here to spend Christmas and New Year. It's a beautiful morning. I wake up early because I want to go to the ocean to see the sun come up. At the ocean the water makes noise like music. The sun comes up, the sky is red, it is so beautiful. A lot of things come into my mind. I thank God for the year 2009. It was a beautiful year and it ends more beautiful because Francina and Rafe and their family are here.

Christmas day we spent together with much happiness. Looking at the kids open their presents, their eyes, they are so happy and I am happy too.

Francina made lasagna for Christmas dinner. After dinner, all together, we went to the pool. It is sunny and warm here, but I think how cold it must be in New York. It is so beautiful to end this year here.

౷

I have been volunteering now for about eight years. I volunteer at three hospitals. It makes me feel so good to help people. They gave me a job called "Transporter." (I have a boss. I haven't had a boss in many, many years. It feels funny.)

My job is to bring patients in wheelchairs to X-ray, or therapy, or help those who are being discharged. I even bring new mothers and their baby down to be discharged. This is so rewarding. It is such a great feeling.

౷

I mentioned before about the Davenport Club. We joined when the kids were young. We have now been members for over 30 years. It was, and still is, a family club. And the family club got bigger! Shawn and John decided to join the club with their family. So, in the summer of 2008, they became members. It was so much fun to go to the club, and see my grandchildren there playing on the beach, playing ball, swimming in the pool, jumping off the diving board.

Ottavio with Owen, Christopher,
and Eric at the Davenport Club pool 2004

During the summer months, Francina would come up from Maryland with the kids to visit, and we would all be at the club enjoying the beach. Many times we stayed and cooked on the beach.

On July 8, 2009, Anna and I celebrated our 40th anniversary. The kids gave us a party on the beach. They decorated the beach, they cooked on the beach. We had a great time! Another celebration and fun time at the club. Another memory.

The following summer, Michelle and Thomas decided to also join the club. So, in the summer of 2010 they too became members. Oh my! I can't believe it. Every day I go to the club and I see four of my grandchildren. Tavia is so cute! She is now one year old. I am so blessed.

At the end of the summer, in the fall of 2010, Michelle and Thomas told us they were expecting another baby. What great news! The family is getting bigger. Then, on May 16, 2011, they had a baby boy. Thomas was born. Another Thomas DeVivo in the family. My father would be so proud. A third generation of Thomas! This is beautiful. I am so happy. I can't believe it. I now have eight grandchildren. We have six grandsons and two granddaughters. Beautiful!

Time passes so fast. The grandchildren are growing so quickly. My life revolves around their lives. We spend holidays together and birthdays, christenings, communions, confirmations, graduations. Happy times and good memories.

Our first grandchild, Owen, who is now 17 years old, graduated from high school in June, 2015. He is planning to go to the University of Delaware to study to be a mechanical engineer. Imagine my grandson in college! I can't believe it.

Eight grandchildren: Jack, Luke, Thomas, Christopher, Tessa, Eric, Owen, and Tavia 2014

After Owen's graduation, on the 4th of July weekend, we celebrated our 46th wedding anniversary and Shawn and John's 17th wedding anniversary. Francina, Rafe and kids came to New York, and we all went out to eat. Michelle and Thomas said Tavia had a surprise for us. Tavia then told us she was going to be a big sister again. We were so happy! Such great news!

So, our little Michael was born on December 22, 2015. Grandchild number nine. We now have seven grandsons and two granddaughters. Our three children all have three children. I am so blessed.

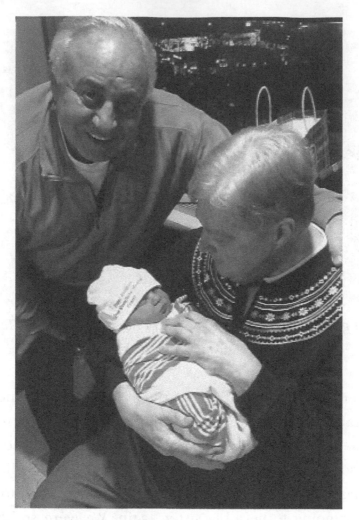

And Michael makes nine 2015

ↄ

We are in Florida for vacation from January to April.
When we first bought our condo I started to play golf. Having
never played, but living on a golf course, I just had to learn.
I took a few lessons, and found out it takes a lot of practice!
I told Anna that "that little ball can drive you crazy". I still

enjoy playing with friends twice a week. I'm getting better, but I will never be a pro! I also play bocce every morning from 8:00 to 11:00 a.m. I think I'm a little better at bocce. I have been playing bocce for a long time, but some days even bocce can be hard.

Ottavio on the golf course in Florida

One morning I came home from playing bocce and looked at Anna. She had a very sad face. I asked her what happened and she said, "I have bad news. Luisa has passed away." I felt very sad and I started to cry. She was my favorite sister. Luisa was very understanding and we communicated very well with each other. I had talked to her a week earlier. We talked about our two sisters, Assunta and Gaetanina, who had passed away and also my brother, Giovanni. My sister said it was her turn to die now, and I said, "If you die, who will I talk to every week? And laugh with?"

Ottavio playing Bocce in Florida

My heart was broken, but I felt God gave me a grandson just two weeks before he took my sister to keep my heart full. I was happy knowing that my mother and father opened the door to heaven for Luisa. After my wife told me about my sister, I went into the bedroom and found a dime on the floor.

My niece, AnnMarie, who was killed in a car accident 25 years ago, sent it to me, I'm sure. She was so beautiful, so sweet, so special. She knows I am always thinking of her.

AnnMarie was the daughter of Anna's brother, Orlando, and his wife, Iris. As a child, she always carried dimes in case she needed to call home. After she died, her family and friends began to find dimes around the house, on the sidewalk, all over the place. Anna found her first dime on the sidewalk one day, she picked it up and put in her pocket. A few weeks later, she learned others who knew AnnMarie were also finding dimes, love notes from AnnMarie. At the cemetery, a couple of months later, I saw a small pile of dimes on her monument. So many love notes.

I also remember my nephew, L.R., who came to Florida on his honeymoon. I took him and his wife, Helen, to dinner to a nice restaurant on the water. We had a good time. L.R and Helen were very happy. We ate dinner, we talked, and enjoyed looking at the red Jupiter Lighthouse.

L.R. became ill a few years ago. He then passed away, joining his cousin AnnMarie in Heaven. The key to this book is to tell people to communicate with each other. To always remember the good times.

I had an idea. I knew a jewelry designer. His name is Michael. I asked Michael if he could make a lighthouse charm in gold. Michael said, "If I make only one, it will be $700.00, but if I make a mold and make four, it would be $200.00 each." I thought, one for Anna, one for L.R.'s mom, Brenda, one for Francina, and one for a good friend, Elinor. I tell this story because when I look at the light house charm, it reminds me of the happy time with L.R and Helen.

One day while we were in Florida, my wife and I were invited to Chick and Gladys's house. Gladys is my sister-in-law Iris's sister. They were having a party, and there were a lot of people at their home. Their son, Chas, was also there. He had been ill and we were so glad to see him. I took him outside and we talked about work and about sports. He was very happy to talk with me. We laughed. Chas was a great guy, with a great smile. He passed away a short time later, but as with all my relatives, he will never be forgotten. This part of the book is very sad, but I know they are all in Heaven together.

cx

AnnMarie Romeo

Chas and Ottavio

LR and Helen on their honeymoon

I am 78 years old, I pray to God to continue to keep me healthy so I can continue to volunteer at the hospital, and help my wife to recover from her surgery.

One day, while I was in a meeting, I got a call from my wife who had gone to her doctor for a physical. She told me she was in an ambulance on her way to the hospital because her doctor thought she was having a stroke. She could not walk.

In the emergency room, they wanted to do an MRI. Anna wanted an open MRI, which the hospital did not have. So we went home. We had an open MRI done at another facility the next day.

After the MRI, we went to see a specialist, who highly recommended that Anna needed surgery right away. She had a very serious condition in her neck. He said that, without surgery, she would not be able to walk. I looked at Anna. The specialist wanted us to see a nerve doctor, who also said she needed the surgery right away.

My children wanted us to see other doctors for another opinion. I said to Anna, "This is your decision. The children are trying to help, but they are confusing." Anna decided to have the surgery right away with the original doctor.

After a four-hour surgery, the doctor came out to tell us that the surgery went well. The children and I went into the room to visit with her. She spent five days in the hospital and a week in rehab. When the doctor gave her the O.K. to go home, it was the best day of my life.

When we went home, I parked next to my "Lucky Tree," the tree that was given to me many years ago by Simon. I feel he is still watching over me.

That's how I want to end this book. I wish everyone in the world to have the same thing that I have because I have my health, I have my wife, I have my children, I have my grandchildren. I have all these beautiful things in the world!

I am a simple man. I like to wish everybody the best in the world.

Ottavio at the Garden of the Gods, Colorado 1995 &
Christopher there (same spot) twenty years later, 2015